Preserves

Preserves

Joanna Farrow

COLLINS & BROWN

First published in Great Britain in 2005 by Collins & Brown Limited

The Chrysalis Building

Bramley Road

London W10 6SP

An imprint of **Chrysalis** Books Group plc

Published in association with The National Magazine Company Limited.
Good Housekeeping is a trade mark of The National Magazine Company Limited.

The Good Housekeeping website address is www.goodhousekeeping.co.uk

1 2 3 4 5 6 7 8 9

British Library Cataloguing-in-Publication Data:
A catalogue record for this book is available from the British Library.

ISBN 1-84340-267-X

Editor: Nicola Hodgson
Designer: Gemma Wilson
Photography: Lucinda Symons
Home economist: Kim Morphew
Proofreader: Fiona Corbridge
Indexer: Margaret Binns

Reproduction by Classicscan, Singapore
Printed and bound by Times Offset, Malaysia

This book was typeset using Gill Sans and Garamond ITC

Note

All values for energy, fat and carbohydrate values given are for 1 heaped tablespoon (25g/1oz). All cooking times and finished amounts are as accurate as possible. These may vary in some cases according to the ripeness and quality of the produce used.

Contents

Introduction

My nanny was a good cook — nothing fancy, just simple food cooked well. She baked on a weekly basis. Fruit tea bread, little fairy cakes and perhaps a Victoria sponge so there was something to offer a friend if they popped by for a cup of tea. The sponges would be filled with her own homemade lemon curd. Eggs came from the neighbour's chickens across the road. Then she'd marry them together with butter, sugar and zesty lemons, stirring them in a bowl over a pan of hot water until the ingredients melded together and thickened. After potting, she'd keep it in the fridge and we'd spread it on toast or crumpets cooked on the open fire. So my love affair with preserving began back then. Raspberry jam — another of Nanny's treats — was simply raspberries cooked with sugar. How much easier could it be? The best came when I discovered chutney that all you do is put the chopped-up ingredients in a pan and simmer away until thick and pulpy.

At *Good Housekeeping*, we know from readers' letters that many of you love preserving, so we hope you'll enjoy this book. From the basic principles — how to choose the best ingredients and what equipment you need — to over 100 recipes, from jams and chutneys to homemade drinks, we're sure you'll find this book invaluable. There are classics such as strawberry and raspberry jam, plus more unusual recipes using exotic fruit, such as the kiwi conserve on page 34. Or for those of you short on time, try one of the microwave recipes (microwave raspberry jam, page 40). For me, the best part is knowing exactly what goes into each jar, then sampling the contents later.

Enjoy!

Emma Marsden
Cookery Editor, *Good Housekeeping*

Equipment

Most of the recipes in this book make small, manageable quantities of preserves. You needn't worry about buying a stack of specialist equipment: regular pots and pans, ladles, spoons, measuring jugs, and kitchen scales are all perfectly adequate for cooking. For potting you simply need to collect an assortment of glass jars, keeping the lids if re-usable. If you're particularly keen to use special equipment, here are some items that it might be worth splashing out on.

Preserving pan

Available in stainless steel, tin-lined copper or lined aluminium, preserving pans should be heavy-based to prevent the contents catching or burning, and wide enough to allow jams, jellies and marmalades to boil up and maintain a 'fast rolling boil' without splashing or spilling all over the cooker. Choose a good-quality preserving pan and it'll last a lifetime, doubling up as a large saucepan on occasions when you're cooking for a crowd. Avoid using unlined preserving pans because the acidic ingredients can react with the metal, and don't use brass or copper pans for pickles and chutneys as the vinegar is highly reactive and will corrode metal, affecting the finished result. A large saucepan makes a good substitute for a preserving pan, provided it's sturdy and has a heavy base. The pan must be of a size that is sufficient to allow the ingredients to boil up (once the sugar has been added, it should be no more than half full). You might need to allow a little longer for boiling because of the reduced surface area.

Jam jars

While it's easy to collect empty jars for your own supply of preserves, you might want to buy new jam jars or other heatproof jars if making preserves as gifts. Jars holding about 450g (1lb) are the most useful.

Bottling jars

These are the wide-necked jars with glass or metal lids, secured by screw bands or clips, sometimes with a thin rubber ring that acts as a seal. They can also be used for sweet preserves, but are particularly suited to chunky pickles and preserves containing whole or large pieces of fruit or vegetables.

Jam jar labels and covers

All you need to cover, seal and label preserves can be bought in small cellophane packs. These will usually contain wax disks to cover the jam, cellophane to go over the top of the jar and elastic bands to secure it. Use metal lids on top of this, which can still be covered attractively with paper or fabric, if you want an extra seal on the preserve.

Long-handled wooden spoon

For stirring preserves in the pan without the risk of getting your fingers too close to the hot ingredients.

Sugar thermometer

Not essential, but saves times when 'testing for a set' when making jams, jellies and marmalades. Boil the jam for slightly less than its recommended setting time, then immerse the thermometer in the pan, without touching the sides. When the temperature reaches 105°C (221°F), the setting point has been reached or almost reached. Because fruits set at slightly different temperatures, use this as a guide and follow it up with one of the tests on page 13.

Nylon sieve

Best for straining large quantities of fruits. Don't use a metal sieve because it might react with the acid in the fruit, affecting the final colour and flavour.

Slotted spoon

Used for skimming off any scum or fruit stones from the surface of the preserve.

Wide-necked preserving funnel

Helps you to fill jam and preserving jars without spilling the mixture all down the sides. Alternatively, pour the mixture into the jars using a heatproof jug.

Jelly bag

A fine-mesh bag that can be suspended (from a handle or the legs of an upturned chair) for straining fruit pulp for jelly-making. Some jelly bags are now available with stands so you can simply leave them on the worksurface.

Large bowl

Useful for brining ingredients for pickling and for straining jelly extract.

Ingredients

Many of the recipes in this book require only fresh fruit and sugar. It is best to make the recipes when the products are plentiful and in season. For example, Seville oranges, which make marmalade, are available from early January. A lot of traditional summer fruits like raspberries and apricots, however, can now be found in supermarkets all year round. All the other ingredients are easy to find in most supermarkets.

Fruit and vegetables

Almost every fruit and vegetable can be preserved in some way. Only use the best-quality, freshest produce available as you won't achieve a well-flavoured preserve from poor ingredients. Wash the produce well and remove any damaged parts before you start, then follow individual recipes for preparation instructions. Most fruit and vegetables only require minimal chopping as they will generally be cooked to a pulp, so don't waste time chopping them into even-sized pieces. For marmalades and preserves containing citrus fruits, use unwaxed fruit if possible or thoroughly scrub with a little washing up liquid if not. Try to use organic fruit and vegetables wherever possible.

Sugar

Sugar is widely used in making preserves, both to flavour and act as a preservative and setting agent. White granulated or caster sugar can be used for jams, conserves, jellies and marmalades; golden sugar makes a slightly darker coloured preserve. Preserving sugar tends to be more expensive but dissolves well, produces less scum on the surface during boiling and gives a clearer preserve. The caramel flavour of light or dark muscovado sugar is good in chutneys, relishes and pickles.

Sugar with pectin

This is a blend of granulated sugar, natural apple pectin and tartaric acid. It is useful when making jams, jellies and conserves with fruits that are naturally low in pectin (see page 12).

Vinegar

Vinegar provides flavour and prevents the growth of micro-organisms in pickles and chutneys. Use red, white, cider or herb-infused vinegars. Ready-made spiced vinegar can be used for additional flavour in chutneys or vegetable pickles, or you can make your own following the recipes on pages 116–7. Alternatively, bring in extra flavour by steeping grated horseradish, strips of orange or lemon peel, or a peeled garlic clove in malt or wine vinegar for one to two weeks before use.

Distilled vinegar has no flavour or colour and is often used for pickled spiced fruits or lighter vegetable pickles.

Salt

Salt is used as a seasoning in many savoury preserves. It acts as a preservative and powerful dehydrator for fruits and vegetables used in pickles, leaving them crisp and extending their storage life. Coarse crystal sea salt is purer and has a stronger flavour than cheaper cooking salt.

Commercial pectin

When making preserves with fruits that are naturally low in pectin, you can aid setting by using commercial pectin. This is available as 'sugar with pectin' (see above) or as bottled liquid pectin, and should be used following the manufacturer's instructions. Alternatively, you can make your own pectin extract. Roughly chop 450g (1lb) whole Bramley apples and cook very gently in a covered pan with 300ml (½ pint) water until pulpy. Strain through a jelly bag (see page 15) and carry out a pectin test (see page 12). Allow 75–150ml (3–5fl oz) to 900g (2lb) low pectin fruit.

Lemon juice

Along with pectin, acid is a vital requirement in jam-, jelly- and marmalade-making. Lemon juice is rich in both these substances and brings out the flavour of the fruit. Allow 2 tablespoons lemon juice to 900g (2lb) fruit with poor setting properties, adding the lemon juice when softening the fruit.

Citric and tartaric acids

Available from the chemist's, these help to extract the pectin from the fruit. Allow ¼ teaspoon to 900g (2lb) of a fruit with poor setting properties. Add to the fruit as it softens.

Spices

Whole and ground spices can be added to pickles and chutneys to add flavour that will mature and mellow during storage.

Whole spices can be tied in a small piece of muslin so they can be removed easily after cooking. Items such as cinnamon sticks can simply be added to the other ingredients and fished out after cooking. Try to use fresh spices wherever possible.

Herbs

Although not widely used, a small quantity of herbs, like bay leaves, rosemary, lavender or thyme are an invaluable addition to some preserves, particularly jellies. Use really fresh, undamaged herbs, preferably ones that have been freshly picked during the morning.

Alcohol

Alcohol prevents the growth of micro-organisms in preserved fruits and drinks. Brandy, rum, gin and orange flavoured liqueurs enhance fruit preserves while vodka is useful in recipes where you don't want the flavour of the alcohol to dominate.

Jams, jellies and marmalades

These preserves are all made following the same basic method – softening fruit with water, boiling it up with sugar and setting it in jars. To set sufficiently the fruits must contain enough pectin, a natural gum-like substance present in fruits to varying degrees, and acid to activate the pectin. The right balance of sugar to fruit is also essential as this gives the preserve its keeping quality. Too little sugar and you run the risk of fermentation, too much and it'll be oversweet.

If the ratio of sugar to fruit is too high it will also affect its natural flavour and may cause crystallization during storage. You can make your own reduced-sugar jam, similar to those available in the shops. Follow the method used for jam, reducing the sugar by no more than 20% or the jam will be runny. As it does not keep well, make in small batches and store in the fridge for up to six weeks.

Pectin

Slightly under-ripe fruit contains more pectin than ripe fruit and fruits that are naturally quite sharp, even when ripe, contain the highest pectin content. Fruits with a low pectin content like strawberries, are usually cooked with a high pectin fruit such as lemon, apple or redcurrant juice or with the aid of commercial pectin, citric or tartaric acid. Fruits that are high in pectin also contain high amounts of acid to activate the pectin, so making and setting preserves using these fruits is the easiest of all.

Testing the pectin content

If making a jam, jelly or marmalade with a medium- or low-pectin fruit, it's worth using the following test to be sure of a good result. Once the fruit is cooked, but before you add the sugar, put 1 teaspoon of the juice into a small dish. When cool, add 1 tablespoon methylated spirit, shake the dish and leave for 1 minute then pour the mixture on to a plate. The consistency

of the juice is a clear indication of how firm the resulting jam will be. If the fruit contains plenty of pectin it will have an almost jelly-like consistency. If very loose or not holding together at all, you will need to add more pectin.

PECTIN CONTENT	FRUIT
HIGH	Cooking apples, crabapples, cranberries, citrus fruit, damsons, gooseberries, redcurrants, blackcurrants, plums (some varieties), quinces.
MEDIUM	Apricots, blackberries, dessert apples, greengages, loganberries, mulberries, raspberries, plums.
LOW	Bananas, cherries, figs, grapes, japonicas, marrows, medlars, melons, nectarines, peaches, pears, pineapples, rhubarb, strawberries.

Sterilizing jars

Prepare the jars in advance so they're ready and waiting to fill. Thoroughly wash new and used jars (soak them in hot water first if necessary to remove old labels).

Oven method: Preheat the oven to 140°C (120°C fan oven) mark 1 and put the upturned jars on a baking sheet in the oven for 10-15 minutes or until completely dry.
Microwave method: Quarter fill four jars with water and arrange in a circle in the microwave. Bring to the boil on HIGH. Remove with oven gloves, pour out the water and invert onto a clean teatowel or kitchen paper.
Dishwasher method: Run the upturned jars through a hot dishwasher cycle.

Testing for a set

This can be done in one of the following ways:

Temperature test: The jam is ready when the temperature registers 105°C (221°F) on a sugar thermometer. Simply immerse the thermometer in the jam shortly before the specified cooking time is completed, keeping it away from the base and sides of the pan. Leave in position until the temperature has been reached. Boil a little longer if necessary.

Saucer test: Drop a spoonful of the jam on to a chilled saucer and leave to cool slightly. Push your finger through the jam: if the surface wrinkles, the jam is ready. Return to the heat and boil a little longer if necessary.

Flake test: Using a large wooden spoon, lift a little of the jam out of the pan. Let it cool slightly then tip the spoon so that the jam drops back into the pan. If it has been boiled for long enough, drops of the syrup will run together along the edge of the spoon and form flakes which will break off sharply. Boil a little longer if necessary.

Filling the jars

When setting point has been reached, turn off the heat and skim off any scum from the surface of the preserve using a slotted spoon. Immediately ladle the jam into the clean, warm jars using a wide-necked funnel if available. Fill the jars right to the neck, as the hot preserve will shrink back slightly on cooling. While the jam is still hot, place a small waxed disc, waxed side down, on the surface. Cover with cellophane jam pot covers and secure with elastic bands. If you forget to cover them while still hot, leave until completely cold as mould might grow on the surface if the jam is covered while warm. Store in a cool, dry place. For long-term storage, cover the jars with screw tops as well.

Making jam

Jams are made by cooking a single fruit (or a mixture of two or more fruits) with sugar to a pulpy consistency that sets on cooling. The high concentration of sugar used in jam making prevents the growth of microorganisms and allows the jam to be stored for up to a year, unless making a reduced-sugar jam (see page 12). Conserves are whole, sometimes chopped, fruits suspended in thick syrup.

1 **Softening the fruit** Once the fruit has been prepared following the appropriate recipe, it'll need gentle cooking before adding any sugar to soften the skin and release the pectin. A muslin bag containing spices, citrus fruit peel and pips can be added to the fruit for extra flavour and pectin. Soft, juicy fruits such as strawberries, raspberries and blackcurrants need no additional water, while firmer fruits like apples and plums need just enough water, to prevent the fruit burning. The simmering time varies depending on the firmness of the fruit used – tough-skinned ones such as gooseberries and quince will take longer than softer fruits. If extra pectin or acid is needed, add to the pan at this stage.

2 **Adding the sugar** If the sugar is warmed in a bowl in the oven before adding it to the softened fruits, it'll dissolve more quickly and speed up the cooking process, but this is not essential. Tip the sugar into the fruit pulp and stir over a low heat until it has completely dissolved i.e. no sugar crystals remain in the bottom of the pan.

3 **Boiling the jam** Once the sugar has dissolved, increase the heat and let the jam bubble until the setting point is reached (see page 13). Boiling times vary according to the fruit used and can take anything from 10 to 25 minutes.

4 **Filling the jars** When the setting point has been reached, turn off the heat and fill the sterilized jars. Pot and cover (see page 13) Store in a cool, dry place.

Tip
If making a jam containing whole strawberries or other pieces of fruit, leave to stand for 15 minutes before potting, to prevent the fruit rising to the top of the jars.

Softening the fruit

Adding the sugar

Making jelly

A jelly is similar to jam except that the fruit pulp is strained overnight before being boiled up with the sugar to make a clear preserve. Although the process is longer than jam-making, the results are thoroughly rewarding and well worth the effort. Fruits with a high pectin content (see page 12) are best for jelly making. Those with a low pectin content are best combined with a high pectin fruit such as redcurrant or apple, or made using sugar with pectin.

1   **Preparing the fruit** Wash the fruit, removing any damaged or bruised parts before weighing it. Don't peel, core or stone fruit: this will all be discarded during straining. Leave small fruits such as blackberries and damsons whole and roughly chop larger fruits such as apples and oranges.

2   **Cooking the fruit** Put the fruit and water in a preserving pan or large heavy-based saucepan and simmer very gently until the fruit is tender. The cooking time will vary considerably depending on the softness of the fruit and can take from 30 minutes to 1½ hours.

3   **Straining the fruit pulp** Scald a jelly bag in boiling water. Suspend the bag from a hook or from the legs of an upturned stool, and position a large bowl underneath to catch the juice. Spoon the pulp into the bag and leave it until the dripping stops. This is best done overnight to extract as much juice as possible. Don't be tempted to squeeze the bag or the jelly will end up cloudy. Once strained, test the juice for pectin content (see page 12).

4   **Adding the sugar** Measure the strained juice into a preserving pan or large saucepan and add the sugar, allowing 450g (1lb) sugar for every 600ml (1pint) juice of high pectin content, and 350g (12oz) sugar for juice with a medium pectin content. Cook over a gentle heat, stirring until the sugar has dissolved. Bring to the boil and boil until the setting point has been reached. Stir in any herbs if you are using any. Test for a set, pot and cover (see page 13).

Tip

For a small quantity of jelly you can use a large plastic sieve with muslin to strain the fruit. If using a very high-pectin fruit a double extraction can be made to increase the final yield. After the first straining, re-cook the dry pulp with a little water and strain again, adding the second batch of juice to the first. Remove all traces of scum from the surface of a jelly before potting by trailing a piece of absorbent kitchen paper over the surface.

Preparing the fruit

Straining the fruit pulp

Making marmalade

Marmalades are made using one or more citrus fruits, occasionally with the addition of another non-citrus fruit, spice or liqueur. The whole fruit is used, including the skin, so cooking times tend to be longer than for jam-making. With any marmalade recipe, you can cut the peel to the thickness you prefer. Because citrus fruits are so high in pectin, marmalades tend to set well so you don't have to bother with pectin tests. Most of the pectin is contained in the pith and skin.

1 **Preparing the fruit** Wash the fruit thoroughly and cut it in half. Squeeze the juice into a preserving pan or large saucepan, reserving the pips. Tie the pips and any pith that comes away from the skins in a square of muslin and add to the pan. Slice the peel, thinly or thickly, depending on personal preference. Add to the pan with the measured water.

2 **Cooking the fruit** This usually takes between one and two hours, depending on the firmness of the peel. Bring to the boil, then reduce the heat and simmer gently until the peel is very soft and falls apart easily. The contents of the pan should be reduced by about half. Lift out the muslin bag with a slotted spoon, squeezing it against the side of the pan to remove as much juice as possible.

3 **Adding the sugar** Stir in the sugar and heat gently until the sugar dissolves. Bring to the boil and boil rapidly until setting point is reached. For most marmalades this takes about 20 minutes. Test for a set, pot and cover as on page 13.

Tip
It's important with marmalades to make sure the peel is very soft and tender before adding the sugar as it won't soften any more once the sugar is added.

Lifting out the muslin bag, squeezing it against the side

When the fruit is cooked, the peel falls apart easily

Making chutney and relish

Chutneys and relishes are made from a mixture of fruit and vegetables cooked with vinegar, sugar and spices. While chutneys tend to be pulpy and mellow, relishes are chunkier because of the shorter cooking time, and tend to have a fresher flavour.

1   **Preparing the ingredients** Chop or slice the ingredients by hand or in a food processor, removing the skin, cores, stalks, seeds etc. Slightly over-ripe fruit and vegetables can be used up without spoiling the finished result.

2   **Cooking the ingredients** Put the ingredients into a preserving pan or large saucepan and bring to the boil. Reduce the heat and cook over the lowest setting, stirring occasionally, until the chutney has thickened and is pulpy. This will take between about 1 and 3 hours depending on the quantity made and type of fruit and vegetables used.

3   **Checking consistency** The mixture is ready when a wooden spoon drawn through the pan leaves a clear channel which very slowly fills up with juice.

4   **Filling the jars** Ladle the chutney into thoroughly clean, warm jars, then cover and label.

Cooking the ingredients

Preparing and covering jars

Chutneys and relishes can be stored in new or used jam jars, or wide-necked preserving jars with rubber seals. Although these must be clean and dry, there's no need to sterilize the jars as the vinegar acts as a strong preservative. Chutneys and relishes must be covered with airtight, vinegar-proof lids as vinegar corrodes metal, which would affect the colour and flavour of the contents during storage. It will also evaporate through jam pot discs and covers. Instead, use jars with plastic, coated metal lids. Used coffee jars and bought pickle jars are ideal.

Checking consistency

Making pickle

Pickles are made using raw or very lightly cooked fruit or vegetables, with vinegar, sugar, spices and other flavourings acting as preservatives. Young, fresh vegetables and firm, ripe fruits retain the best flavour and texture during storage. Most vegetables for pickling are first brined with salt for one or two days. Some, such as onions, are wet brined, while those containing large amounts of water are dry brined to draw out excess water which would dilute the flavour and reduce storage time.

Vegetable pickles

1 **Preparing the vegetables** Wash well, removing any damaged parts, then peel, trim and cut up as in chosen recipe.

2a **Wet brining** Put the whole or cut vegetables in a large bowl and pour over the brine solution. Place a plate on top to keep the vegetables submerged in the liquid, and leave to stand overnight. (Some vegetables, such as onions are brined once and then drained and brined again.)

2b **Dry brining** Layer up the vegetables, with plenty of salt in a large bowl. Cover and leave for 24 hours. After brining, rinse off the salt thoroughly, as any excess will spoil the flavour of the finished pickle. This is best done by immersing the vegetables in plenty of cold water, draining in a large colander, then repeating the process twice more.

3 **Cooking the vegetables** Some vegetables are cooked briefly prior to bottling. Bring a large saucepan of water to the boil. Tip in the rinsed vegetables and return to the boil. Cook for the time stated, then drain and refresh under cold water to prevent further cooking and retain the colour.

4 **Filling the jars** Neatly pack the vegetables into the prepared jars (see page 8), filling the jars right up to the neck but not so tightly that the vegetables are crushed. Drain off any water that has gathered in the base of the jars.

5 **Adding the vinegar** Pour the plain or flavoured vinegar over the vegetables, making sure the top layer is submerged by about 1cm (½in) as vinegar evaporates during storage and any uncovered vegetables will discolour and spoil. Cover and seal the jars as for chutneys and relishes.

Wet brining

Dry brining

Fruit pickles

1 **Preparing the fruit** Wash the fruit, discarding any damaged parts, and cut up as in chosen recipe.

2 **Heating the vinegar** Put the vinegar, sugar and spices into a large saucepan and heat gently until dissolved. At this stage, add the prepared fruit (if it is to be cooked) and cook gently for the stated time. Take care not to overcook the fruit, bearing in mind that it'll soften further as it cools.

3 **Filling the jars** Pack the fruit into the jars and add the vinegar, making sure the fruit is completely submerged. Cover and seal the jars as for chutneys and relishes.

Making sauces and cordials

Some sauces and cordials, like apple sauce and orange, lemon and ginger cordial need sterilizing once potted or bottled to prolong their storage life. Before making the preserve, collect plenty of bottles or jars and screw-topped oil and vinegar bottles. Try to find bottles or jars of an equal height so that when they're placed in the pan as shown below, they are all sterilized equally. Small wide-necked sauce bottles are ideal for apple sauce, but again make sure they're of a similar size.

Sterilizing sauces and cordials

For sterilization, use bottles with metal or plastic screw caps or rubber stoppers. Make sure the bottles are thoroughly clean beforehand, washing them by hand or running them through a dishwasher cycle. Next, heat the bottles in the oven at 140°C (120°C Fan oven) mark 1 and boil the caps in water for 10–15 minutes.

Once you have made your sauce or cordial, fill screw-topped bottles to just under 2.5cm (1in) from the top to leave room for expansion on heating. Seal with screw caps or rubber stoppers. Put the bottles in a deep pan, padded on the base and between the bottles with newspaper. Fill the pan with warm water to the base of the caps or stoppers, then raise the temperature and simmer for 30 minutes. (This should register 77°C/170°F on a thermometer if you have one.) Remove the bottles and tighten any screw caps used. Store in a cool, dark place.

Once the bottles have been filled, sterilize them in a deep pan, padded on the base with newspaper.

Jams and conserves

Jams are a delicious way of preserving the flavour of seasonal fruits,
particularly those that are only around for a short time, such as apricots,
cherries and gooseberries. Provided suitable storage conditions exist, you can
make enough jam to keep you going right through the year, until the next
fresh supply of fruit is available. Most jams and conserves can be kept for up
to a year. Smaller quantities of jam can also be prepared conveniently in the
microwave, or an uncooked soft fruit jam can be made for storage in the
freezer. Reduced sugar jams give a less sweet, more intensely fruity flavour but
must be kept in the fridge and used within six weeks. Jams can be made using
one type of fruit or a mixture, for example, several soft summer fruits, and
herbs and spices can be added to complement their natural flavours. In a
conserve, fruit is also preserved by cooking with sugar but it is not 'set' like
jam. Instead, whole or chunky pieces of fruit are suspended in a deliciously
thick syrup. Strawberries, raspberries and rhubarb make excellent conserves,
retaining a flavour that's much closer to the original taste of the fruit.
Conserves can be used in much the same way as jam, and are also delicious
spooned over ice-cream, yogurt and creamy desserts.

Raspberry jam

1   Put the fruit in a preserving pan and simmer very gently in its own juice for about 10 minutes, stirring carefully from time to time, until the fruit is really soft.

2   Remove the pan from the heat and add the sugar, stirring until dissolved, then add the butter and boil for about 10–15 minutes or until setting point is reached.

3   Remove any scum with a slotted spoon, then pot and cover.

Variation: loganberry jam
Follow the above recipe, using loganberries instead of raspberries.

900g (2lb) raspberries, washed
900g (2lb) sugar
a knob of butter

PREPARATION TIME: 10 minutes
COOKING TIME: 25 minutes
MAKES: 1.3kg (2¾lb)
PER SERVING: 75 cals, 0g fat, 19g carbohydrate

Strawberry jam

1   Put the strawberries in a preserving pan with the sugar and lemon juice. Heat gently until the sugar has dissolved, stirring frequently.

2   Bring to the boil and boil steadily for about 4 minutes or until setting point is reached.

3   Remove from the heat and remove any scum with a slotted spoon. Leave to stand for 15–20 minutes.

4   Stir the jam gently, then pot and cover.

900g (2lb) strawberries, hulled and
    washed
1kg (2.2lb) sugar with pectin
juice of ½ lemon

PREPARATION TIME: 10 minutes, plus standing
COOKING TIME: 10 minutes
MAKES: 1.8kg (4lb)
PER SERVING: 60 cals, 0g fat, 15g carbohydrate

Summer fruit jam

1   Put all the fruit in a bowl and sprinkle over 30ml (2tbsp) of the fructose. Cover and leave overnight in the refrigerator.

2   Transfer the fruit to a heavy-based saucepan and add 50ml (2fl oz) water. Simmer gently until tender, then add the remaining fructose and stir until dissolved.

3   Bring to the boil and boil for 15–20 minutes or until setting point is reached. Remove any scum with a slotted spoon.

4   Leave the jam to cool for 5 minutes, then pot and cover. Store in the refrigerator.

450g (1lb) strawberries, hulled and washed
100g (4oz) redcurrants, strings removed and washed
100g (4oz) raspberries, washed
275g (10oz) fructose

PREPARATION TIME: 10 minutes, plus overnight soaking
COOKING TIME: 25 minutes
MAKES: 555g (1¼lb)
PER SERVING: 55 cals, 0g fat, 15g carbohydrate

Black cherry jam

1   Put the cherries in a preserving pan with the sugar, orange rind and orange juice. Heat gently until the sugar has dissolved, then simmer until the fruit is soft. Bring to the boil and boil rapidly for 4 minutes or until setting point is reached.

2   Remove any scum with a slotted spoon, then pot and cover.

900g (2lb) black cherries, washed and stoned
1kg (2¼lb) sugar with pectin
grated rind and juice of 2 oranges

PREPARATION TIME: 10 minutes
COOKING TIME: 20 minutes
MAKES: 1.4kg (3lb)
PER SERVING: 80 cals, 0g fat, 21g carbohydrate

Plum jam

1   Halve the plums if large and put in a preserving pan or large, heavy-based saucepan with 300ml (½ pint) water. Simmer gently for about 20 minutes or until the fruit is really soft and the contents of the pan are well reduced.

2   Remove the pan from the heat, add the sugar and stir until dissolved. Add the butter, bring to the boil and boil rapidly for 10 minutes or until setting point is reached.

3   Using a slotted spoon, remove the stones and any scum from the surface of the jam. Pot and cover.

900g (2lb) ripe plums, washed,
    halved and stoned
900g (2lb) sugar
a knob of butter

PREPARATION TIME: 10 minutes
COOKING TIME: 30 minutes
MAKES: 1.4kg (3lb)
PER SERVING: 70 cals, trace amounts of fat, 18g carbohydrate

Blackcurrant jam

1   If time, gently prick each currant and place in a bowl with the sugar. Cover and leave overnight.

2   Transfer the fruit and sugar to a saucepan, bring slowly to the boil and boil for 3 minutes or until setting point is reached.

3   Remove the pan from the heat and leave for about 30 minutes, until a skin begins to form. Stir gently to distribute the fruit, then pot and cover.

900g (2lb) blackcurrants, strings
    washed and removed
1.4kg (3lb) sugar

PREPARATION TIME: 10 minutes, plus standing
COOKING TIME: 10 minutes
MAKES: 2.3kg (5lb)
PER SERVING: 65 cals, 0g fat, 17g carbohydrate

Blackberry and apple jam

1   Bring the apples and 150ml (¼ pint) water to the boil in a preserving pan or large, heavy-based saucepan. Cook gently for 5 minutes until soft. Add the lemon juice and berries and simmer for 5 minutes or until the berries begin to break up.

2   Add the sugar, stirring until all the sugar dissolves. Stir in the butter and bring to the boil. Boil rapidly for about 15 minutes until setting point is reached. Stir in the liqueur, if using.

3   Remove any scum with a slotted spoon. Leave to cool for 15 minutes, then pot and cover.

450g (1lb) cooking apples, peeled,
     cored and diced
2tbsp lemon juice
450g (1lb) blackberries
600g (1lb 4oz) sugar
3tbsp blackberry liqueur (optional)
a knob of butter

PREPARATION TIME: 10 minutes
COOKING TIME: 25 minutes
MAKES: 1kg (2¼ lb)
PER SERVING: 70 cals, trace amounts
of fat, 18g carbohydrate

Mulberry and apple jam

1   Put the mulberries in a preserving pan with 300ml (½ pint) water and simmer gently for about 20 minutes or until soft and pulpy.

2   Put the apples in a saucepan with 300ml (½ pint) water and simmer gently for about 20 minutes or until soft and pulpy.

3   Add the apples to the mulberries and stir in the sugar. Continue stirring until the sugar has dissolved, then add the butter and boil for about 10 minutes or until setting point is reached.

4   Remove any scum with a slotted spoon, then pot and cover.

1.4kg (3lb) mulberries, washed
450g (1lb) cooking apples, peeled,
     cored and sliced (prepared
     weight)
1.6kg (3½ lb) sugar
a knob of butter

PREPARATION TIME: 10 minutes
COOKING TIME: 55 minutes
MAKES: 2.3kg (5lb)
PER SERVING: 75 cals, trace amounts
of fat, 20g carbohydrate

Pear jam

1   Peel, core and chop the pears, reserving the peel and cores. Put the peel and cores in a saucepan with the lemon rind and 150ml (¼ pint) water and boil for 10 minutes.

2   Strain and pour the liquid into a preserving pan and add the pear flesh and lemon juice. Simmer gently for 25–30 minutes or until the pears are tender.

3   Remove the pan from the heat, add the sugar and stir until dissolved. Add the butter, bring to the boil and boil for 5–10 minutes.

4   Remove the pan from the heat, add the pectin, then boil for a further minute. Remove any scum with a slotted spoon and allow the jam to cool slightly before potting and covering in the usual way.

1.4kg (3lb) cooking or firm eating pears
grated rind and juice of 2 lemons
1.1kg (2½ lb) sugar
a knob of butter
half a 227ml (8fl oz) bottle of commercial pectin

PREPARATION TIME: 10 minutes, plus standing
COOKING TIME: 50 minutes
MAKES: 900g (2lb)
PER SERVING: 130 cals, trace amounts of fat, 35g carbohydrate

Blueberry bay jam

1   Put the blueberries in a preserving pan with 150ml (¼ pint) water, the lemon juice and the bay leaves. Simmer gently for 10–15 minutes or until the fruit is just beginning to turn pulpy.

2   Remove the pan from the heat, add the sugar and stir gently until dissolved. Add the butter, bring to the boil and boil rapidly for 4 minutes or until setting point is reached.

3   Remove any scum with a slotted spoon, allow the jam to stand for 3–4 minutes, then remove the bay leaves. Pot and cover.

900g (2lb) blueberries, washed
6tbsp lemon juice
3 bay leaves
1.1kg (2½ lb) sugar with pectin
a knob of butter

PREPARATION TIME: 10 minutes, plus standing
COOKING TIME: 25 minutes
MAKES: 2.4kg (5lb)
PER SERVING: 50 cals, trace amounts of fat, 13g carbohydrate

Apricot jam

1   Crack a few of the reserved apricot stones with a weight, nutcracker or hammer, take out the kernels and blanch in boiling water for 1 minute, then drain. Peel away the papery skins from the kernels.

2   Put the apricots, lemon juice, apricot kernels and 450ml (¾ pint) water in a preserving pan and simmer for about 20 minutes or until soft and the contents of the pan are well reduced.

3   Take the pan off the heat and add the sugar, stirring until dissolved. Add the butter and boil rapidly for about 15 minutes or until setting point is reached.

4   Remove any scum with a slotted spoon, then pot and cover.

900g (2lb) apricots, washed, halved and stoned (reserving a few stones)
juice of 1 lemon
900g (2lb) sugar
a knob of butter

PREPARATION TIME: 20 minutes
COOKING TIME: 35 minutes
MAKES: 1.4kg (3½lb)
PER SERVING: 40 cals, trace amounts of fat, 10g carbohydrate

Peach and raspberry jam

1   Crack the peach stones with a nutcracker or hammer, take out the kernels and tie them in a piece of muslin. Put the fruit in a preserving pan with the muslin bag and 150ml (¼ pint) water. Bring to the boil and simmer gently for about 30 minutes or until the fruit is tender. Remove the muslin bag, squeezing well.

2   Remove the pan from the heat, add the sugar and stir until dissolved. Add the butter and boil for about 15 minutes or until setting point is reached.

3   Remove any scum with a slotted spoon, then pot and cover.

900g (2lb) fresh peaches, skinned, stoned and chopped (prepared weight)
900g (2lb) raspberries, washed
1.4kg (3lb) sugar
a knob of butter

PREPARATION TIME: 15 minutes
COOKING TIME: 45 minutes
MAKES: 2.3kg (5lb)
PER SERVING: 65 cals, trace amounts of fat, 17g carbohydrate

Elderflower gooseberry jam

1   Tie the elderflowers in a piece of muslin. Put the gooseberries in a preserving pan with 300ml (½ pint) water and the elderflower bundle. Simmer gently for about 20 minutes or until the fruit is really soft and reduced, mashing it to a pulp with a wooden spoon and stirring from time to time to prevent sticking.

2   Remove the pan from the heat, add the sugar and stir until dissolved, then add the butter. Bring to the boil and boil rapidly for about 10 minutes or until setting point is reached.

3   Remove any scum with a slotted spoon. Remove the muslin bag, then pot and cover.

5 elderflower heads, cut close to the stem and washed
700g (1lb 8oz) gooseberries (slighter under-ripe), topped, tailed and washed
700g (1lb 8oz) sugar
a knob of butter

PREPARATION TIME: 20 minutes
COOKING TIME: 30 minutes
MAKES: 1kg (2¼lb)
PER SERVING: 75 cals, 0g fat, 19g carbohydrate

Rose petal jam

1   Remove the petals from the rose blossoms. Snip off the white bases of the petals.

2   Cut the petals into small pieces, but not too finely. Put in a bowl and add 225g (8oz) of the sugar. Cover and leave overnight. This will extract the scent and darken the petals.

3   Pour 1.1 litres (2 pints) water and the lemon juice into a heavy-based saucepan and stir in the remaining sugar. Heat gently until the sugar has dissolved, but do not boil.

4   Stir the rose petals into the sugar syrup and simmer gently for 20 minutes. Bring to the boil and boil for about 5 minutes or until thick. (This jam is not brought to setting point.) Pot and cover.

225g (8oz) deep red, heavily-scented rose blooms, picked in full bloom
450g (1lb) sugar
juice of 2 lemons

PREPARATION TIME: 15 minutes, plus standing
COOKING TIME: 30 minutes
MAKES: 450g (1lb)
PER SERVING: 100 cals, trace amounts of fat, 26g carbohydrate

Melon and ginger jam

1 Put the prepared melon in a bowl, sprinkle with about 450g (1lb) of the sugar and leave to stand overnight.

2 Crush or 'bruise' the ginger with a rolling pin or weight to release the flavour from the fibres, and tie it in a piece of muslin with the lemon rind.

3 Put the muslin bag in a preserving pan with the melon and lemon juice. Simmer gently for 30 minutes, then remove the pan from the heat and add the remaining sugar, stirring until dissolved.

4 Add the butter and boil gently for about 30 minutes or until setting point is reached.

5 Remove the muslin bag and any scum with a slotted spoon, then pot and cover.

1.8kg (4lb) honeydew melon,
    seeded, skinned and diced
    (prepared weight)
1.8kg (4lb) sugar
25g (1oz) fresh root ginger
thinly pared rind and juice of
    3 lemons
a knob of butter

PREPARATION TIME: 15 minutes, plus standing
COOKING TIME: 1 hour
MAKES: 2.3kg (5lb)
PER SERVING: 80 cals, trace amounts of fat, 22g carbohydrate

Honey-pineapple jam

1   Crush the pineapple thoroughly with a rolling pin or masher and put it in a preserving pan with the lemon juice and honey. Mix well, bring to the boil and simmer for 20 minutes, stirring occasionally.

2   Remove the pan from the heat and stir in the pectin. Bring to the boil for 1 minute and remove any scum with a slotted spoon. Pot and cover.

1.4kg (3lb) ripe pineapple, peeled, cored and chopped
juice of 1 lemon
700 g (1lb 8oz) thick honey
half a 227ml (8fl oz) bottle of commercial pectin

PREPARATION TIME: 15 minutes
COOKING TIME: 25 minutes
MAKES: 1.1kg (2½lb)
PER SERVING: 60 cals, 0g fat, 15g carbohydrate

Fresh fig jam

1   Put the fruit in a heavy-based saucepan with the lemon rind and juice. Simmer gently for about 30 minutes or until the fruit is quite tender.

2   Remove the pan from the heat, add the sugar and stir until dissolved. Add the butter, bring to the boil and boil rapidly for 10 minutes or until setting point is reached.

3   Remove any scum with a slotted spoon, then pot and cover.

450g (1lb) fresh figs, washed and sliced
225g (8oz) cooking apples, peeled, cored and sliced
grated rind of 1 lemon
juice of 3 lemons
450g (1lb) sugar
a knob of butter

PREPARATION TIME: 10 minutes
COOKING TIME: 40 minutes
MAKES: 900g (2lb)
PER SERVING: 70 cals, trace amounts of fat, 18g carbohydrate

Kiwi conserve

1   Slice the fruit thickly and place in a bowl in layers with the sugar. Cover and leave for 24 hours.

2   Transfer the fruit to a saucepan and bring slowly to the boil, stirring until the sugar dissolves. Boil rapidly for 5 minutes. Leave to cool for 15 minutes, then pot and cover.

900g (2lb) kiwi fruit, peeled
900g (2lb) sugar

PREPARATION TIME: 10 minutes, plus standing
COOKING TIME: 10 minutes
MAKES: 1.4kg (3lb)
PER SERVING: 70 cals, 0g fat, 18g carbohydrate

Kumquat conserve

1   Prick the kumquats all over with a needle. Place the fruit in a bowl in layers with the sugar. Cover and leave for 24 hours.

2   Transfer the fruit to a saucepan and bring to the boil slowly, stirring until the sugar has dissolved. Boil rapidly for 10 minutes.

3   Remove any pips that have risen to the surface and stir in the brandy. Leave to cool for 15 minutes, then pot and cover.

900g (2lb) kumquats, washed
900g (2lb) sugar
6tbsp brandy

PREPARATION TIME: 15 minutes, plus standing
COOKING TIME: 20 minutes
MAKES: 1.8kg (4lb)
PER SERVING: 55 cals, 0g fat, 14g carbohydrate

Strawberry conserve

1 Put the strawberries in a large bowl in layers with the sugar. Cover and leave for 24 hours.

2 Put the strawberries and sugar in a preserving pan and heat gently, stirring until the sugar dissolves. Bring to the boil and boil rapidly for 5 minutes.

3 Return the mixture to the bowl, cover and leave in a cool place for a further 2 days.

4 Return the mixture to the pan again and boil rapidly for 10 minutes. Leave to cool for 15 minutes, then pot and cover in the usual way.

Note
Raspberries and loganberries can be conserved in the same way.

1.4kg (3lb) strawberries, hulled
1.4kg (3lb) sugar

PREPARATION TIME: 15 minutes, plus standing
COOKING TIME: 25 minutes
MAKES: 1.4kg (3lb)
PER SERVING: 100 cals, 0g fat, 28g carbohydrate

Raspberry kirsch conserve

1 Put the raspberries and sugar in separate ovenproof dishes. Heat in the oven at 180°C (350°F) mark 4 for 15 minutes.

2 Turn the raspberries and sugar into a large bowl and stir for a few minutes. Leave to stand for 20 minutes. Repeat the stirring and leaving to stand procedure three times.

3 Stir the kirsch into the conserve, then pot and cover. Store in a cool, dark place for at least 3 months before using.

450g (1lb) raspberries, washed
450g (1lb) sugar
1tbsp kirsch

PREPARATION TIME: 10 minutes, plus standing
COOKING TIME: 15 minutes
MAKES: 900g (2lb)
PER SERVING: 50 cals, 0g fat, 14g carbohydrate

Rhubarb and ginger conserve

1   Put the rhubarb in a bowl in layers with the sugar. Cover and leave overnight.

2   Put the rhubarb and sugar in a preserving pan. Crush or 'bruise' the root ginger slightly, using a rolling pin or hammer, and tie in a piece of muslin. Add to the pan and bring slowly to the boil, stirring, until the sugar has dissolved. Boil rapidly for 15 minutes.

3   Add the stem ginger to the pan and boil for a further 5 minutes.

4   Remove the muslin bag and any scum with a slotted spoon, then pot and cover.

1.1kg (2½ lb) rhubarb, trimmed, washed and cut into small pieces
1.1kg (2½ lb) preserving sugar
25g (1oz) fresh root ginger
100g (4oz) stem ginger, roughly chopped

PREPARATION TIME: 15 minutes, plus standing
COOKING TIME: 30 minutes
MAKES: 2.4kg (5lb)
PER SERVING: 45 cals, 0g fat, 12g carbohydrate

Uncooked freezer jam

1   Put the fruit in a large bowl and crush it very lightly with a fork.

2   Stir in the sugar and lemon juice and leave for about 2–3 hours at room temperature, stirring occasionally, or until the sugar has dissolved.

3   Gently stir in the pectin and continue stirring for a further 2 minutes.

4   Pour the jam into small plastic containers, leaving a little space at the top to allow for expansion. Cover and leave at room temperature for a further 24 hours.

5   Label the containers and freeze.

6   To serve, thaw at room temperature for about 1 hour.

Note
This jam has a soft set similar to a conserve. It will keep for up to six months in a freezer.

700g (1lb 8oz) raspberries or
    strawberries, hulled
700g (1lb 8oz) caster sugar
2tbsp lemon juice
half a 227ml (8fl oz) bottle of
    commercial pectin

PREPARATION TIME: 15 minutes, plus standing
MAKES: 1.4kg (3lb)
PER SERVING: 55 cals, 0g fat, 14g carbohydrate

Microwave raspberry jam

1   Put the frozen fruit in a large heatproof bowl and microwave on HIGH for 4 minutes to thaw. Stir several times with a wooden spoon to ensure even thawing.

2   Add the lemon juice and sugar. Mix well and microwave on HIGH for 5 minutes or until the sugar has dissolved, stirring several times.

3   Microwave on HIGH for 13 minutes or until setting point is reached, stirring occasionally. Pot and cover.

450g (1lb) frozen raspberries
2tbsp lemon juice
450g (1lb) sugar

PREPARATION TIME: 10 minutes
COOKING TIME: 22 minutes
MAKES: 700g (1½lb)
PER SERVING: 65 cals, 0g fat, 18g carbohydrate

Microwave rhubarb and ginger jam

1   Chop the rhubarb into short even-sized lengths and arrange in a large heatproof bowl in layers with the sugar. Pour over the lemon juice. Cover and leave in a cool place overnight.

2   Uncover the rhubarb and add the root ginger. Microwave on HIGH for 5 minutes or until the sugar has dissolved, stirring twice.

3   Remove the root ginger, add the crystallized ginger and microwave on HIGH for 14 minutes or until setting point is reached. Pot and cover.

450g (1lb) rhubarb, trimmed
   (prepared weight)
450g (1lb) sugar
juice of 1 lemon
2.5cm (1in) piece of dried root
   ginger, bruised
50g (2oz) crystallized ginger,
   chopped

PREPARATION TIME: 15 minutes, plus standing
COOKING TIME: 21 minutes
MAKES: 450g (1lb)
PER SERVING: 110 cals, 0g fat, 29g carbohydrate

Microwave crushed strawberry jam

1 Put the strawberries in a large heatproof bowl with the lemon juice. Cover and microwave on HIGH for 5 minutes or until the strawberries are soft, stirring frequently.

2 Lightly crush the strawberries with a potato masher. Add the sugar and stir well. Microwave on LOW for 15 minutes or until the sugar has dissolved, stirring frequently.

3 Microwave on HIGH for 20–25 minutes or until setting point is reached. Stir in the butter.

4 Allow the jam to cool slightly, then pot and cover.

450g (1lb) strawberries, hulled
3 tbsp lemon juice
450g (1lb) sugar
a knob of butter

PREPARATION TIME: 10 minutes, plus standing
COOKING TIME: about 45 minutes;
MAKES: about 700g (1½lb)
PER SERVING: 70 cals, trace amounts of fat, 18g carbohydrate

Jellies

Jellies make fabulous additions to the storecupboard and are great for sharing with family and friends. Like jams, they're perfect for serving with bread and scones but are slightly more versatile. Serve them as a sauce accompaniment to roast meat and game dishes, or stir a spoonful of fruit jelly into a meat gravy or sauce to give a subtle sweetness, gloss and flavour that complements the meat. Herbs such as mint, lavender or thyme make pretty, fragrant additions to jellies, particularly if you're making them as gifts. There is no yield quantity given for the jellies in this chapter because this depends so much on the ripeness of the fruit, evaporation of water during cooking, and length of time allowed for straining. As a rough guide, for each 450g (1lb) sugar added, you'll make about 700g (1lb 8oz) of jelly. As with jams and conserves, jellies can be stored for up to a year.

Blackberry or bramble jelly

1 Put the fruit in a preserving pan with 600ml (1 pint) water. Bring to the boil and simmer gently for 30 minutes or until very tender.

2 Spoon the fruit pulp into a jelly bag or cloth attached to the legs of an upturned stool, and leave to strain into a large bowl for at least 12 hours.

3 Discard the pulp remaining in the jelly bag. Measure the extract and return it to the preserving pan with 450g (1lb) sugar for each 600ml (1 pint) extract.

4 Heat gently, stirring, until the sugar has dissolved, then bring to the boil and boil rapidly for 1 minute or until setting point is reached. Remove any scum with a slotted spoon, then pot and cover.

900g (2lb) blackberries or brambles, washed
sugar with pectin

PREPARATION TIME: 25 minutes, plus standing
COOKING TIME: 40 minutes
PER SERVING: 60 cals, 0g fat, 15g carbohydrate

Four-fruit jelly

1 It is not necessary to string the redcurrants. Put all the fruit in a preserving pan with the lemon juice and 600ml (1 pint) water. Simmer gently for about 1 hour or until the fruit is really soft and pulpy. Stir from time to time to prevent sticking.

2 Spoon the fruit pulp into a jelly bag or cloth attached to the legs of an upturned stool, and leave to strain into a large bowl for at least 12 hours.

3 Discard the pulp remaining in the jelly bag. Measure the extract and return it to the preserving pan with 450g (1lb) sugar for each 600ml (1 pint) extract.

4 Heat gently, stirring, until the sugar has dissolved, then bring to the boil and boil rapidly for about 10 minutes or until setting point is reached. Remove any scum with a slotted spoon, then pot and cover.

450g (1lb) redcurrants, washed
450g (1lb) raspberries, washed
450g (1lb) Morello or May Duke cherries, washed
450g (1lb) strawberries, washed
4tbsp lemon juice
sugar

PREPARATION TIME: 25 minutes, plus standing
COOKING TIME: 1 hour 20 minutes
PER SERVING: 50 cals, 0g fat, 14g carbohydrate

Redcurrant and apple jelly

1   There is no need to remove the stalks from the redcurrants. Remove any bruised portions from the apples and slice them without peeling or coring.

2   Put the fruit in a preserving pan and add 1.4 litres (2½ pints) water. Simmer very gently for about 1 hour or until the fruit is thoroughly cooked and pulpy. Stir from time to time to prevent sticking.

3   Spoon the fruit pulp into a jelly bag or cloth attached to the legs of an upturned stool, and leave to strain into a large bowl for at least 12 hours.

4   Discard the pulp remaining in the jelly bag. Measure the extract and return it to the preserving pan with 450 g (1lb) sugar for each 600ml (1 pint) extract.

5   Heat gently, stirring, until the sugar has dissolved, then boil rapidly for 8–10 minutes or until setting point is reached. Remove any scum with a slotted spoon, then pot and cover.

900g (2lb) redcurrants, washed
900g (2lb) cooking apples, washed
sugar

PREPARATION TIME: 25 minutes, plus standing
COOKING TIME: 1 hour 20 minutes
PER SERVING: 50 cals, 0g fat, 14g carbohydrate

Crabapple jelly

1   Cut the crabapples into quarters without peeling or coring and put them in a preserving pan with the cloves and 1.7 litres (3 pints) water. Bring to the boil and simmer gently for about 1½ hours or until the fruit is soft and pulpy, adding a little more water if necessary. Stir from time to time to prevent sticking.

2   Spoon the fruit pulp into a jelly bag or cloth attached to the legs of an upturned stool, and leave to strain into a large bowl for at least 12 hours.

3   Discard the pulp remaining in the jelly bag. Measure the extract and return it to the pan with 450g (1lb) sugar for each 600ml (1 pint) extract. Heat gently, stirring, until the sugar has dissolved, then boil rapidly for about 10 minutes or until setting point is reached.

4   Remove any scum with a slotted spoon, then pot and cover.

2.5kg (5½lb) crabapples, washed
6 cloves
sugar

PREPARATION TIME: 25 minutes, plus standing
COOKING TIME: 1 hour 50 minutes
PER SERVING: 70 cals, 0g fat, 18g carbohydrate

Damson and apple jelly

1 Remove any bruised or damaged portions from the apples and roughly chop them into large chunks without peeling or coring. Put the apples and damsons in a heavy-based saucepan with 600ml (1 pint) water and simmer gently for about 30 minutes or until the fruit is really soft and pulpy. Stir from time to time to prevent sticking.

2 Spoon the fruit pulp into a jelly bag or cloth attached to the legs of an upturned stool, and leave to strain into a large bowl for at least 12 hours.

3 Discard the pulp remaining in the jelly bag. Measure the extract and return it to the preserving pan with 450g (1lb) sugar for each 600ml (1 pint) extract.

4 Heat gently, stirring, until the sugar has dissolved, then bring to the boil and boil rapidly for about 10 minutes or until setting point is reached. Remove any scum with a slotted spoon, then pot and cover.

700g (1lb 8oz) cooking apples, washed
400g (14oz) damsons, washed
sugar

PREPARATION TIME: 25 minutes, plus standing
COOKING TIME: 50 minutes
PER SERVING: 60 cals, 0g fat, 16g carbohydrate

Cranberry and apple jelly

1 Remove any bruised or damaged portions from the apples, then roughly chop them without peeling or coring.

2 Put the apples and cranberries in a preserving pan with sufficient water to cover them and simmer gently for 45 minutes to 1 hour or until the fruit is really soft and pulpy. Stir from time to time to prevent sticking.

3 Spoon the pulp into a jelly bag or cloth attached to the legs of an upturned stool, and leave to strain into a large bowl for at least 12 hours.

4 Discard the pulp remaining in the jelly bag. Measure the extract and return it to the preserving pan with 450g (1lb) sugar for each 600ml (1 pint) extract. Bring slowly to the boil, stirring, until the sugar has dissolved, then boil rapidly for about 10 minutes or until setting point is reached.

5 Remove any scum with a slotted spoon, then pot and cover.

1.4kg (3lb) cooking apples, washed
900g (2lb) cranberries, washed
granulated sugar

PREPARATION TIME: 25 minutes, plus standing
COOKING TIME: 1 hour 20 minutes
PER SERVING: 70 cals, 0g fat, 18g carbohydrate

Apple and mint jelly

1   Remove any bruised or damaged portions from the apples and roughly chop them into thick chunks, without peeling or coring.

2   Put the apples in a preserving pan with 600ml (1 pint) water and the mint sprigs. Bring to the boil, then simmer gently for about 40 minutes or until soft and pulpy. Stir from time to time to prevent sticking. Add the vinegar and boil for a further 5 minutes.

3   Spoon the apple pulp into a jelly bag or cloth attached to the legs of an upturned stool, and leave to strain into a large bowl for at least 12 hours.

4   Discard the pulp remaining in the jelly bag. Measure the extract and return it to the preserving pan with 450g (1lb) sugar for each 600ml (1 pint) extract.

5   Heat gently, stirring, until the sugar has dissolved, then boil rapidly for about 10 minutes or until setting point is reached.

6   Remove any scum with a slotted spoon, then stir in the chopped mint. Allow to cool slightly, stir well to distribute the mint, then pot and cover.

Variations: herb jellies
Other fresh herbs, such as rosemary, parsley, sage, lavender and thyme, can be used instead of mint. Serve these herb jellies with roast meats – rosemary jelly with lamb; parsley jelly with gammon; sage jelly with pork; and lavender or thyme jelly with poultry.

1.1kg (2lb 8oz) cooking apples,
    such as Bramleys
a few large sprigs of fresh mint
600ml (1 pint) distilled white
    vinegar
sugar
4 level tbsp chopped fresh mint

PREPARATION TIME: 25 minutes,
plus standing
COOKING TIME: 1 hour 15 minutes
PER SERVING: 50 cals, 0g fat, 14g
carbohydrate

Orange and thyme jelly

1 Slice the oranges and lemons, then cut the slices into quarters. Put in a preserving pan with 60ml (4tbsp) chopped thyme and 2.8 litres (5 pints) water. Bring to the boil, then simmer gently for about 1½ hours or until the fruit is soft. Stir from time to time to prevent sticking.

2 Spoon the fruit pulp into a jelly bag or cloth attached to the legs of an upturned stool, and leave to strain into a large bowl for at least 12 hours.

3 Discard the pulp remaining in the jelly bag. Measure the extract and return it to the preserving pan with 450g (1lb) sugar for each 600ml (1 pint) extract.

4 Heat gently, stirring, until the sugar has dissolved, then bring to the boil and boil rapidly for about 15 minutes or until setting point is reached. Remove any scum with a slotted spoon, then stir in the remaining chopped thyme.

5 Allow the jelly to cool slightly, then stir well to distribute the thyme. Pot and cover.

1.8kg (4lb) oranges, washed
450g (1lb) lemons, washed
8 level tbsp chopped fresh thyme
sugar

PREPARATION TIME: 25 minutes, plus standing
COOKING TIME: 1 hour 40 minutes
PER SERVING: 70 cals, 0g fat, 18g carbohydrate

Currant and port jelly

1   There is no need to remove the currants from their stalks. Put the currants in a preserving pan with 600ml (1 pint) water and simmer gently for about 30 minutes or until the fruit is really soft and pulpy. Stir from time to time to prevent sticking.

2   Spoon the fruit pulp into a jelly bag or cloth attached to the legs of an upturned stool, and leave to strain into a large bowl for at least 12 hours.

3   Discard the pulp remaining in the jelly bag. Measure the extract and return it to the preserving pan with 450g (1lb) sugar for each 600ml (1 pint) extract.

4   Heat gently, stirring, until the sugar has dissolved, then boil rapidly for about 15 minutes or until setting point is reached.

5   Stir in the port, remove any scum with a slotted spoon, then pot and cover in the usual way.

1.4kg (3lb) red or blackcurrants
sugar
45ml (3tbsp) port

PREPARATION TIME: 20 minutes, plus standing
COOKING TIME: 55 minutes
PER SERVING: 70 cals, 0g fat, 18g carbohydrate

Sweet cider jelly

1   Put the cider, orange rind and rosemary in a large saucepan. Bring slowly to the boil and reduce the heat.

2   Add the sugar to the pan and heat gently, stirring, until dissolved. Add the pectin and bring to a fast, rolling boil. Boil hard for 1 minute. Strain through a nylon sieve, then pot and cover in the usual way.

1.1 litres (2 pints) sweet apple cider
thinly pared rind of 2 oranges
15ml (1tbsp) chopped fresh
**   rosemary**
1.4kg (3lb) sugar
227ml (8fl oz) bottle of commercial
**   pectin**

PREPARATION TIME: 10 minutes
COOKING TIME: 15 minutes
PER SERVING: 60 cals, 0g fat, 15g carbohydrate

Marmalades

Marmalade is usually made in winter when citrus fruits are at their best. Although we mainly use marmalade at breakfast time, it makes a tangy addition to sponge cakes, puddings and sauces. Bitter Seville oranges are considered the best for marmalade but are only available in January and February, so if you particularly want to use Seville oranges but don't have time to make marmalade, freeze them whole for a later date. Allow an additional ten per cent fruit if making from frozen as a small amount of pectin is lost during freezing. Sweet oranges are available throughout the year and can also be used for marmalade, but they tend to give a cloudier appearance as the pith does not turn translucent. Some of the tastiest marmalades are made using a combination of fruits such as tangerine and grapefruit, or orange and apple.

Lemon marmalade

1   Halve the lemons and squeeze out the juice and pips. Cut each 'cap' of peel in half and, with a sharp knife, remove the membrane and some of the pith from the peel. Tie the membrane, pith and pips in a piece of muslin.

2   Slice the peel to the desired thickness and put it in a preserving pan with the juice, muslin bag and 1.1 litres (2 pints) water. Bring to the boil, then simmer gently for about 1¼ hours or until the peel is soft and the contents of the pan reduced by half.

3   Remove the muslin bag, squeezing out as much juice as possible and letting it run back into the pan.

4   Add the sugar, stir until dissolved, then bring to the boil and boil rapidly for about 15 minutes or until setting point is reached. Remove any scum with a slotted spoon, leave the marmalade to stand for about 15 minutes, then stir to distribute the peel. Pot and cover in the usual way.

450g (1lb) ripe, juicy lemons, washed
700g (1lb 8oz) sugar

PREPARATION TIME: 40 minutes, plus standing
COOKING TIME: 1 hour
MAKES: 1.4kg (3lb)
PER SERVING: 65 cals, 0g fat, 17g carbohydrate

Lime marmalade

1   Put the limes in the preserving pan or large saucepan and add 1.7 litres (3 pints) water. Cover with a tight-fitting lid and simmer for 1½ to 2 hours or until the fruit is very soft.

2   Remove the fruit from the pan with a slotted spoon and slice very thinly (using a knife and fork), discarding the pips and reserving any juice. Return the sliced fruit and juice to the pan.

3   Add the sugar and stir until it has dissolved, then bring to the boil and boil rapidly for about 15 minutes or until setting point is reached. Remove any scum with a slotted spoon, leave the marmalade to stand for about 15 minutes, then stir gently to distribute the fruit. Pot and cover.

700g (1lb 8oz) limes, washed
1.4kg (3lb) sugar

PREPARATION TIME: 25 minutes, plus standing
COOKING TIME: 2 hours 25 minutes
MAKES: 2.3kg (5lb)
PER SERVING: 60 cals, 0g fat, 16g carbohydrate

Tangerine jelly marmalade

1   All together, the fruit should weigh about 1.3 kg (2¾ lb). Peel the tangerines and cut the peel into fine shreds. Tie the shreds in a piece of muslin.

2   Peel the grapefruit and lemon and cut up the peel up. Roughly chop the flesh of all the fruit, reserving the juice, and put the flesh, juice and peel in a preserving pan with the muslin bag.

3   Add the citric acid and 2.8 litres (5 pints) water to the pan, and simmer for about 2 hours or until the fruit is soft. Remove the muslin bag after 30 minutes, squeezing it well and allowing the juice to run back into the pan.

4   Untie the muslin bag, place the tangerine peel in a sieve, wash under cold water, then drain and reserve.

5   Spoon the pulped fruit into a jelly bag or cloth attached to the legs of an upturned stool, and leave to strain into a large bowl for about 2 hours.

6   Discard the pulp remaining in the jelly bag. Pour the extract into a clean preserving pan and add the sugar. Heat gently, stirring, until the sugar has dissolved. Bring to the boil, stir in the reserved tangerine peel and boil rapidly for 10 minutes or until setting point is reached. Remove any scum with a slotted spoon, leave the marmalade to stand for 15 minutes, then stir to distribute the shreds. Pot and cover.

900g (2lb) tangerines, washed
1 large grapefruit, washed
1 lemon, washed
1 level tsp citric acid
1.4kg (3lb) sugar

PREPARATION TIME: 30 minutes, plus standing
COOKING TIME: 1 hour 20 minutes
MAKES: 2.3kg (5lb)
PER SERVING: 60 cals, 0g fat, 17g carbohydrate

Seville orange marmalade

1   Halve the oranges and squeeze out the juice and pips. Tie the pips, and any extra membrane that has come away during squeezing, in a piece of muslin.

2   Slice the orange peel thinly or thickly, as preferred, and put it in a preserving pan with the fruit juices, muslin bag and 1.1 litres (2 pints) water. Simmer gently for about 2 hours or until the peel is really soft and the liquid reduced by about half.

3   Remove the muslin bag, squeezing it well and allowing the juice to run back into the pan. Add the sugar.

4   Heat gently, stirring until the sugar has dissolved, then bring to the boil and boil rapidly for about 15 minutes or until setting point is reached. Remove any scum with a slotted spoon, then pot and cover.

Variation: whisky marmalade
Follow the recipe for Seville orange marmalade. When setting point is reached, remove any scum with a slotted spoon, then stir in 50ml (2fl oz) whisky. Leave to stand for about 15 minutes, then stir to distribute the peel. Pot and cover.

450g (1lb) Seville oranges, washed
juice of lemon
900g (2lb) sugar

PREPARATION TIME: 25 minutes
COOKING TIME: 2 hours 25 minutes
MAKES: 1.4kg (3lb)
PER SERVING: 60 cals, 0g fat, 17g carbohydrate

Ginger and grapefruit jelly marmalade

1   Cut the grapefruit into quarters. Chop finely, using a sharp knife, or the slicing blade of a food processor.

2   Put the grapefruit and root ginger in a preserving pan and add 2.8 litres (5 pints) water. Bring to the boil, half cover and boil gently for about 1 hour or until the fruit is very soft and the contents of the pan reduced to a thick pulp (there should be little free liquid).

3   Spoon the contents of the pan into a jelly bag or cloth attached to the legs of an upturned stool, and leave to strain into a large bowl for at least 12 hours.

4   Discard the pulp remaining in the jelly bag. Measure the extract (there should be about 1.7 litres/3 pints) and return to the preserving pan.

5   Add 450g (1lb) sugar and 25g (1oz) finely shredded stem ginger for each 600ml (1 pint) extract. Heat gently, stirring, until the sugar has dissolved.

6   Bring to the boil and boil rapidly for about 10 minutes or until setting point is reached. Remove any scum with a slotted spoon, leave the marmalade to stand for 10–15 minutes to allow the jelly to thicken sufficiently to suspend the ginger, then pot and cover.

5 large grapefruit (about 1.8kg/4lb), washed
2.5cm (1in) piece of fresh root ginger, peeled and thinly sliced
granulated sugar
stem ginger in syrup, drained

PREPARATION TIME: 30 minutes, plus standing
COOKING TIME: 1 hour 20 minutes
MAKES: 1.8kg (4lb)
PER SERVING: 75 cals, 0g fat, 20g carbohydrate

Four-fruit processor marmalade

1   Wash all the fruit well. Quarter the citrus fruit and cut each quarter across into three pieces. Slice very thinly by hand with a sharp knife, or using the slicing disc of a food processor. Reserve the pips.

2   Peel, quarter and core the apples. Reserve the peel and thinly slice the flesh. Tie the pips, apple peel and cores in a piece of muslin.

3   Put all the sliced fruit in a preserving pan and add 2 litres (3½ pints) water and the muslin bag. Bring to the boil, then simmer gently for about 2 hours or until the peel is very soft and the contents of the pan reduced by half. Stir occasionally. Remove the muslin bag, squeezing it well and allowing the juice to run back into the pan.

4   Add the sugar to the pan, stirring until it has dissolved.

5   Bring to the boil and boil rapidly for 8–10 minutes or until setting point is reached. Remove any scum with a slotted spoon, leave the marmalade to stand for about 15 minutes, then stir to distribute the peel. Pot and cover.

1 grapefruit (about 350g/12oz)
2 large sweet oranges
    (about 700g/1lb 8oz)
2 large lemons (about 450g/1lb)
350g (12oz) cooking apples
1.4kg (3lb) sugar

PREPARATION TIME: 25 minutes, plus standing
COOKING TIME: 2 hours 20 minutes
MAKES: 2.3kg (5lb)
PER SERVING: 65 cals, 0g fat, 17g carbohydrate

Microwave orange marmalade

1 Pare the rind from the oranges, avoiding the white pith. Shred or chop the rind and set aside. Put the fruit pith, flesh and pips in a food processor and chop until the pips are broken.

2 Put the chopped mixture and lemon juice in a large heatproof bowl and add 900ml (1½ pints) boiling water. Microwave on HIGH for 15 minutes.

3 Strain the mixture through a sieve into another large bowl and press the cooked pulp until all the juice is squeezed out. Discard the pulp. Stir the shredded rind into the hot juice and microwave on HIGH for 15 minutes or until the rind is tender, stirring occasionally. Stir in the sugar until dissolved.

4 Microwave on HIGH for about 10 minutes, stirring once during cooking, until setting point is reached. Stir in the butter, then remove any scum with a slotted spoon. Leave to cool for 15 minutes, then pot and cover the jam in the usual way.

900g (2lb) Seville oranges
juice of 2 lemons
900g (2lb) sugar
a knob of butter

PREPARATION TIME: 25 minutes, plus standing
COOKING TIME: about 40 minutes;
MAKES: about 1.1kg (2½lb)
PER SERVING: 90 cals, trace amounts of fat, 23g carbohydrate

Curds and cheeses

Fruit curds are made by blending fresh, tangy fruits with eggs and butter to make a silky-smooth topping for serving with bread and scones, or to be used as a cake filling. Fruit curds will only keep for a short time, so they're best made in small quantities. They can be stored in a cool place for up to one month or in the fridge for up to three months. Slow, gentle cooking is the key to success, as too high a heat will curdle the mixture. Once cooked, strain the curd through a sieve, then pot and cover as on pages 12–13. Fruit cheeses are firm textured, intensely fruity preserves, often served as an accompaniment to meat, poultry, game or cheese. They're usually made from abundant fruits such as apples, blackberries and damsons as a large quantity of fruit makes a relatively small amount. When cooking fruit cheese, its consistency determines its readiness. A wooden spoon drawn through the mixture should leave a clear trail on the base of the pan. For this reason use a good, heavy-based one so the thick fruit pulp doesn't stick or burn. Pot and cover as on pages 12–13 or set them in small, lightly oiled moulds so they can be turned out and served with cheese. Store for up to three or four months in jars or a week if set in moulds.

Raspberry curd

1 Put the raspberries, apples, orange rind and orange juice in a saucepan. Bring to the boil, then simmer for 20 minutes or until the fruit is soft.

2 Using a wooden spoon, press the fruit pulp through a nylon sieve into the top of a double saucepan or a deep, heatproof bowl standing over a pan of simmering water. Add the eggs, butter and sugar.

3 Heat gently, stirring, until the sugar has dissolved. Continue heating gently, stirring frequently, for 35–40 minutes or until the curd is thick enough to coat the back of a wooden spoon.

4 Strain, pot and cover the curd.

350g (12oz) raspberries, washed
225g (8oz) cooking apples, peeled, cored and chopped
grated rind and juice of 1 orange
4 eggs, beaten
100g (4oz) butter, cut in small pieces
350g (12oz) caster sugar

PREPARATION TIME: 30 minutes
COOKING TIME: 1 hour
MAKES: 700g (1½ lb)
PER SERVING: 95 cals, 14g fat, 15g carbohydrate

Blueberry curd

1 Put the fruit and 15ml (1tbsp) water in a heavy-based saucepan, cover and cook gently until tender. Press through a fine sieve.

2 Return the fruit purée to the saucepan and add the butter and sugar. Heat gently, stirring frequently, to dissolve the sugar and melt the butter.

3 Beat the eggs together in a bowl, then strain into the hot mixture. Heat gently, stirring, until thick enough to coat the back of a wooden spoon.

4 Strain, pot and cover the curd. Once opened, store in the refrigerator and use within 1 month.

225g (8oz) blueberries, washed
50g (2oz) butter, cut in small pieces
225g (8oz) caster sugar
3 eggs, size 3

PREPARATION TIME: 20 minutes
COOKING TIME: 25 minutes
MAKES: 450g (1lb)
PER SERVING: 90 cals, 3g fat, 14g carbohydrate

Cranberry lemon cheese

1   Place the cranberries in a large heavy-based saucepan. Add the pared lemon rind, 45ml (3tbsp) lemon juice and 1.3 litres (2¼ pints) water.

2   Bring slowly to the boil, then cover and simmer for about 30 minutes or until very soft.

3   Using a wooden spoon, press the berries and juices through a nylon sieve and measure the purée. Return the purée to the pan and add 350g (12oz) sugar for every 600ml (1 pint) purée.

4   Heat gently, stirring, until the sugar has completely dissolved, then bring to the boil and boil, stirring frequently, for about 40–50 minutes or until a spoon drawn across the bottom of the pan leaves a clear line through the mixture. Take care as the preserve will spit as it reduces. Spoon away the scum from the top.

5   Pot and cover the cheese or, if preferred, set in small dishes or moulds.

1kg (2¼ lb) cranberries unwashed
thinly pared rind and juice of
   2 lemons
sugar

PREPARATION TIME: 25 minutes
COOKING TIME: 1 hour 20 minutes
MAKES: 1.4kg (3lb)
PER SERVING: 20 cals, 0g fat, 6g carbohydrate

Orange curd

1   Place all the ingredients in the top of a double saucepan or in a deep heatproof bowl standing over a pan of simmering water.

2   Heat gently, stirring, for about 20 minutes or until the sugar has dissolved and the mixture has thickened enough to coat the back of a wooden spoon.

3   Strain, pot and cover the curd. Keeps for 1 month refrigerated.

**finely grated rind and juice of
  1 large orange**
1tbsp lemon juice
125g (4½oz) caster sugar
50g (2oz) unsalted butter, cubed
2 large egg yolks, beaten

PREPARATION TIME: 15 minutes
COOKING TIME: 15 minutes
MAKES: 400g (14oz)
PER SERVING: 130 cals, 7g fat, 18g carbohydrate

Lemon curd

1   Place all the ingredients in the top of a double saucepan or in a deep heatproof bowl standing over a pan of simmering water.

2   Stir until the sugar has dissolved and continue heating gently, without boiling, for about 20 minutes or until the curd is thick enough to coat the back of a wooden spoon.

3   Strain the curd into jars and cover.

Note
Home-made lemon curd should be made in small quantities as it only keeps for about 1 month. Store in a cool place.

Variation: lime curd
Make as above using the grated rind and juice of five large ripe, juicy limes.

**grated rind and juice of 4 medium
  ripe, juicy lemons**
4 eggs
**100g (4oz) butter, cut in small
  pieces**
350g (12oz) caster sugar

PREPARATION TIME: 20 minutes
COOKING TIME: 25 minutes
MAKES: 700g (1½lb)
PER SERVING: 90 cals, 4g fat, 14g carbohydrate

Blackberry cheese

1   Place the blackberries and apples in a large saucepan or preserving pan
with 600ml (1 pint) water. Bring to the boil and simmer gently for about
30 minutes or until the blackberries are just tender.

2   Using a wooden spoon, press the fruit pulp through a nylon sieve and
measure the purée. Return the purée to the pan and add 350g (12oz)
sugar for each 600ml (1 pint) purée.

3   Heat gently, stirring, until the sugar has dissolved, then bring to the boil and
boil for about 30 minutes or until the mixture is so thick that the wooden
spoon leaves a clean line through the mixture when drawn across the
bottom of the pan.

4   Pot and cover the cheese or, if preferred, set in small dishes or moulds.

900g (2lb) blackberries, washed
450g (1lb) cooking apples, peeled,
   cored and diced
sugar

PREPARATION TIME: 25 minutes;
COOKING TIME: 1 hour 15 minutes
MAKES: 900g (2lb)
PER SERVING: 50 cals, 0g fat, 13g
carbohydrate

Damson cheese

1   Place the fruit in a saucepan, cover with water and simmer gently for 15–20
minutes or until the fruit is very soft. Scoop out the stones with a slotted
spoon as they come to the surface.

2   Using a wooden spoon, press the fruit pulp through a nylon sieve and
measure the purée.

3   Return the purée to the pan and add 350g (12 oz) sugar for each 600ml
(1 pint) purée. Heat gently, stirring, until the sugar has dissolved, then bring
to the boil and boil gently, stirring frequently, for 30–40 minutes or until the
mixture is so thick that the wooden spoon leaves a clean line through the
mixture when drawn across the bottom of the pan.

4   Pot and cover the cheese or, if preferred, set in several small dishes or
moulds.

1.4kg (3lb) damsons, washed
sugar

PREPARATION TIME: 25 minutes
COOKING TIME: 1 hour 10 minutes
MAKES: 1.4kg (3lb)
PER SERVING: 35 cals, 0g fat, 19g
carbohydrate

Variation: gooseberry cheese
Make as above using 1.4kg (3lb) gooseberries and 150ml (¼ pint) water.

Apple cheese

1   Chop the apples, without peeling or coring, and put them in a large saucepan. Add just enough water to cover and simmer gently for about 1 hour or until the apples are very soft and pulpy.

2   Using a wooden spoon, press the apple pulp through a nylon sieve and measure the purée. Return the purée to the pan and add the spices and 450g (1lb) sugar for each 600ml (1 pint) purée.

3   Heat gently, stirring, until the sugar has dissolved, then bring to the boil and boil gently, stirring frequently, for 30–45 minutes or until the mixture is so thick that the wooden spoon leaves a clean line through it when drawn across the bottom of the pan.

4   Pot and cover the cheese or, if preferred, set in several small dishes or moulds.

1.4kg (3lb) cooking apples,
    windfalls or crabapples, washed
½ level tsp ground cinnamon
½ level tsp ground cloves
sugar

PREPARATION TIME: 30 minutes
COOKING TIME: 2 hours
MAKES: 1.4 kg (3lb)
PER SERVING: 95 cals, 0g fat, 25g carbohydrate

Quince cheese

1   Chop the quinces without peeling or coring, put them in a large saucepan and add just enough water to cover. Simmer gently for about 30 minutes or until the fruit is very soft.

2   Using a wooden spoon, press the fruit pulp through a nylon sieve and measure the purée. Return the purée to the pan and add 450g (1lb) sugar for each 600ml (1 pint) purée.

3   Heat gently, stirring, until the sugar has dissolved, then bring to the boil and boil gently, stirring frequently, for 30–40 minutes or until the mixture is so thick that the wooden spoon leaves a clean line through it when drawn across the bottom of the pan.

4   Pot and cover the cheese or, if preferred, set in several small dishes or moulds.

1.4kg (3lb) quinces, washed
sugar

PREPARATION TIME: 25 minutes
COOKING TIME: 1 hour 20 minutes
MAKES: 1.4kg (3lb)
PER SERVING: 90 cals, 0g fat, 24g carbohydrate

Microwave lemon and grapefruit curd

1   Put the fruit rind and juice in a large heatproof bowl. Using a wooden spoon, beat in the eggs and sugar. Add the butter and stir well.

2   Microwave on HIGH for 7 minutes or until thickened, whisking occasionally to ensure even thickening.

3   Remove the bowl from the cooker and whisk for about 5 minutes or until the curd cools and thickens.

4   Strain, pot and cover the curd.

**finely grated rind and juice of
  2 lemons**
**finely grated rind and juice of
  1 large grapefruit**
4 eggs
225g (8oz) caster sugar
100g (4oz) unsalted butter, diced

PREPARATION TIME: 15 minutes
COOKING TIME: 7 minutes
MAKES: 900g (2lb)
PER SERVING: 60 cals, 3g fat, 7g carbohydrate

Chutneys and relishes

The best chutneys and relishes are chunky and full of vibrant flavour — either hot and spicy or more mellow, and are perfect for enhancing a meal of cold meats, patés and cheeses. The wide range of fruits and vegetables used means that these preserves can be made at almost any time of year, although the abundance of ingredients such as apples, marrows, tomatoes and pumpkins in early autumn makes this the perfect time for chutney-making. Chutneys and relishes are incredibly easy to make as they don't rely on accurate boiling, temperature testing or setting to achieve good results. The only watchpoint is the consistency, which should be neither too watery nor too dry (see page 17). Unless stated otherwise in the recipe, chutneys and relishes will keep for up to a year in a cool, dry place and most are best stored for two to three months before eating so the flavours have a chance to mingle and mature.

Simple apple chutney

1   Put the apples, onions, sultanas or raisins, lemon rind and juice, sugar and vinegar in a preserving pan or large heavy-based saucepan.

2   Heat gently, stirring, until the sugar has dissolved, then bring to the boil. Reduce the heat and simmer, uncovered, for about 35 minutes, stirring occasionally, until the mixture is thick and pulpy, with no excess liquid remaining. If the mixture starts to dry out before the fruit and vegetables are tender, add 3–4 tbsp water and continue cooking.

3   Spoon the chutney into clean, dry warmed jars, cover and seal.

Variation: gooseberry chutney
Follow the recipe above, replacing the apples with 700g (1½ lb) gooseberries, topped, tailed and washed.

700g (1½ lb) cooking apples, peeled, cored and diced
700g (1½ lb) onions, skinned and chopped
225g (8oz) sultanas or seedless raisins
grated rind and juice of 1 lemon
350g (12oz) demerara sugar
300ml (½ pint) malt vinegar

PREPARATION TIME: 20 minutes
COOKING TIME: 35 minutes;
MAKES: 1.4kg (3lb)
PER SERVING: 45 cals, trace amounts of fat, 12g carbohydrate

Cranberry and apple chutney

1   Put the cinnamon stick, allspice berries and cumin seeds in a piece of muslin, tie with string and put in a preserving pan or large, heavy-based saucepan.

2   Add the cranberries, apples, onions, sugar and vinegar and bring to the boil. Reduce the heat and simmer very slowly, uncovered, stirring occasionally, for around 1 hour 30 minutes or until the mixture is thick and pulpy. Remove the bag of spices.

3   Spoon the chutney into jars, cover and seal. Use within three months.

1 cinnamon stick
1 level tsp allspice berries, crushed
1 level tsp cumin seeds
1kg (1lb 2oz) cranberries
1kg (1lb 2oz) Granny Smith apples, peeled, cored and diced
450g (1lb) onions, chopped
500g (1lb 2oz) light muscovado sugar
284ml bottle distilled malt vinegar

PREPARATION TIME: 30 minutes
COOKING TIME: 1 hour 45 minutes
MAKES: 1.4kg (3lb)
PER SERVING: 50 cals, 0g fat, 12g carbohydrate

Aubergine and apple chutney

1   Place the aubergines, tomatoes, apples, onion and garlic in a preserving pan or large, heavy-based saucepan and add the raisins, brown sugar, salt and vinegar.

2   Tie the pickling spice in a piece of muslin and add to the pan.

3   Bring to the boil, then simmer uncovered, stirring occasionally, for about 1 hour or until the ingredients are soft and the contents of the pan well reduced.

4   Take out the bag of spices. Spoon the chutney into jars, cover and seal.

350g (12oz) aubergines, roughly chopped

450g (1lb) tomatoes, skinned and chopped

225g (8oz) cooking apples, peeled, cored and sliced

175g (6oz) onion, skinned and chopped

1 garlic clove, skinned and crushed

100g (4oz) seedless raisins

175g (6oz) dark brown soft sugar

1 level tsp salt

300ml (½ pint) distilled vinegar

2 level tsp whole pickling spice

PREPARATION TIME: 25 minutes
COOKING TIME: 1 hour
MAKES: 1.4kg (3lb)
PER SERVING: 20 cals, trace amounts of fat, 5g carbohydrate

Marrow and tomato chutney

1   Finely crush the peppercorns and allspice in a pestle and mortar, or use the end of a rolling pin in a bowl.

2   Put all the ingredients in a preserving pan or large, heavy-based saucepan. Heat gently, stirring, until the sugar has dissolved. Bring to the boil and boil steadily for about 50 minutes or until reduced by half. (This chutney will be a little more liquid than usual.) Stir occasionally to prevent sticking.

3   Cool the chutney slightly, then spoon into jars, cover and seal.

2 level tsp black peppercorns

2 level tsp whole allspice berries

1.4kg (3lb) marrow, peeled, seeded and cut into 1cm (½ in) chunks

450g (1lb) ripe tomatoes, skinned and roughly chopped

225g (8oz) onions, skinned and roughly chopped

2 garlic cloves, skinned and roughly chopped

2 level tsp salt

2 level tsp ground ginger

700g (1lb 8oz) sugar

750ml (1¼ pint) cider vinegar

PREPARATION TIME: 20 minutes
COOKING TIME: 1 hour
MAKES: about 1.6–1.8kg (3½–4 lb)
PER SERVING: 45 cals, trace amounts of fat, 12g carbohydrate

Spiced tomato chutney

1   Put all the ingredients in a large, heavy-based saucepan or preserving pan and stir together. Bring slowly to the boil, stirring from time to time to make sure the sugar dissolves.

2   Simmer gently for 1–1½ hours, stirring occasionally, or until it becomes thick and jam-like.

3   Spoon the chutney into jars, cover and seal. Store for at least 1 month and eat within 3 months.

2 onions, finely chopped

3 garlic cloves, crushed

2 red peppers, halved, deseeded and finely chopped

1 red chilli, deseeded and diced

1kg (2lb 3½oz) ripe tomatoes, chopped

450ml (¾ pint) malt or white wine vinegar

350g (12oz) soft light brown sugar

100g (3½oz) raisins

1 level tsp black mustard seeds

2 level tsp smoked paprika

1 cinnamon stick

½ level tsp ground cloves

PREPARATION TIME: 20 minutes
COOKING TIME: 1–1½ hours
MAKES: 1.1 kg (2½ lb)
PER SERVING: 50 cals, trace amounts of fat, 11g carbohydrate

Green tomato chutney

1   Place all the ingredients in a preserving pan or large, heavy-based saucepan. Bring to the boil, reduce the heat and simmer gently for about 2 hours, stirring occasionally, until the ingredients are tender and reduced to a thick pulpy consistency. Remove the ginger.

2   Spoon the chutney into jars, cover and seal.

450g (1lb) cooking apples, peeled, cored and minced

225g (8oz) onions, skinned and minced

1.4kg (3lb) green tomatoes, thinly sliced

225g (8oz) sultanas

225g (8oz) demerara sugar

2 level tsp salt

450ml (¾ pint) malt vinegar

4 small pieces of dried root ginger

½ level tsp cayenne pepper

1 level tsp mustard powder

PREPARATION TIME: 20 minutes
COOKING TIME: 2 hours
MAKES: 1.4kg (3lb)
PER SERVING: 35 cals, trace amounts of fat, 9g carbohydrate

Beetroot chutney

1 Place all the ingredients in a preserving pan and heat gently, stirring occasionally, for about 1 hour or until the sugar has dissolved. Bring to the boil and simmer gently, uncovered, stirring occasionally, for about 2½ hours or until no excess liquid remains and the mixture is thick and pulpy.

2 Spoon the chutney into clean, dry, warmed jars, cover and seal.

700g (1½ lb) raw beetroot, peeled and chopped

450g (1lb) cooking apples, peeled, cored and chopped

225g (8oz) onions, skinned and chopped

175g (6oz) seedless raisins

750ml (1¼ pint) malt vinegar

500g (1lb 2oz) granulated sugar

1 level tbsp ground ginger

juice of 1 lemon

PREPARATION TIME: 25 minutes
COOKING TIME: 1 hour
MAKES: 1.4kg (3lb)
PER SERVING: 50 cals, trace amounts of fat, 13g carbohydrate

Pumpkin chutney

1 Cut the pumpkin flesh into 1cm (½ inch) cubes and put in a preserving pan with all the other ingredients.

2 Heat gently, stirring, until the sugar has dissolved, then bring to the boil and simmer gently, uncovered, for about 1 hour, stirring occasionally, especially towards the end of the cooking time, until no excess liquid remains and the mixture is thick and pulpy.

3 Spoon the chutney into jars, cover and seal.

900g (2lb) pumpkin, peeled, cored and seeded (prepared weight)

450g (1lb) tomatoes, skinned and roughly chopped

450g (1lb) onions, skinned and roughly chopped

1 garlic clove, skinned and crushed

50g (2oz) sultanas

700g (1½ lb) light brown soft sugar

600ml (1 pint) white wine vinegar

1 level tsp ground allspice

1 level tsp salt

1 level tsp freshly ground black pepper

PREPARATION TIME: 20 minutes
COOKING TIME: 1 hour
MAKES: 2.3kg (5lb)
PER SERVING: 35 cals, trace amounts of fat, 19g carbohydrate

Spiced pepper chutney

1   Place the peppers in a preserving pan or large, heavy-based saucepan with the onions, tomatoes, apples, sugar, allspice and vinegar. Tie the peppercorns and mustard seeds in a piece of muslin and add to the pan.

2   Heat gently, stirring, until the sugar has dissolved. Bring to the boil and simmer, uncovered, over a medium heat for about 1½ hours, stirring occasionally, until soft, pulpy and well reduced. Remove the muslin bag.

3   Spoon the chutney into jars, cover and seal.

3 red peppers, washed, seeded and finely chopped

3 green peppers, washed, seeded and finely chopped

450g (1lb) onions, skinned and sliced

450g (1lb) tomatoes, skinned and chopped

450g (1lb) cooking apples, peeled, cored and chopped

225g (8oz) demerara sugar

1 level tsp ground allspice

450ml (16fl oz) malt vinegar

1 level tsp peppercorns

1 level tsp mustard seeds

PREPARATION TIME: 25 minutes
COOKING TIME: 1½ hours
MAKES: 1.6kg (3½)
PER SERVING: 20 cals, trace amounts of fat, 5g carbohydrate

Coconut-tamarind chutney

1   Put all the ingredients in a mixing bowl and stir well to combine. Cover and chill for several hours to allow the flavours to develop.

2   Transfer to a small jar or serving dish and store in the fridge for up to 3 days.

125g (4½oz) freshly-grated coconut

1 garlic clove, crushed

1 very small onion, grated

1 level tbsp tamarind paste

2 level tbsp natural yogurt

1 tsp olive oil

½ level tsp salt

¼ level tsp pepper

PREPARATION TIME: 15 minutes
MAKES: 175g (6oz)
PER SERVING: 120 cals, 11g fat, 4g carbohydrate

Chilli chutney

1   Put half the tomatoes into a food processor or blender. Cut chillies in half (scooping out and discarding seeds), then roughly chop and add to the blender with the garlic and ginger. Blend to a purée and transfer to a heavy-based saucepan.

2   Crush or bruise the lemongrass and cut in half. Tie the cut halves together with string, then add to the pan with the star anise, sugar and vinegar.

3   Bring mixture to the boil, add the remaining tomatoes, then reduce the heat. Cook gently for 45–50 minutes, stirring occasionally and skimming off any foam, until the mixture has thickened and reduced slightly. Remove the star anise and lemongrass.

4   Spoon the chutney into jars. Cover and seal. Chill and use within 1 month.

900g (2lb) very ripe tomatoes, roughly chopped
8 medium red chillies
6 garlic cloves, crushed
5cm (2 inches) fresh ginger, grated
1 lemongrass stalk, trimmed with outer layer removed
1 star anise
550g (1lb 4oz) golden caster sugar
200ml (7fl oz) red wine vinegar

PREPARATION TIME: 25 minutes
COOKING TIME: 50–55 minutes
MAKES: about 900g (2lb)
PER SERVING: 65 cals, trace amounts of fat, 17g carbohydrate

Spiced rhubarb and orange chutney

1   Put the rhubarb, orange zest, onions, vinegar, sugar and raisins in a preserving pan or large heavy-based saucepan. Tie the spices in a piece of muslin and add to the pan.

2   Heat gently, stirring until the sugar has dissolved, then bring to the boil. Reduce the heat and simmer, uncovered, for about 1 hour, stirring occasionally until the mixture is thick and pulpy and no excess liquid remains. Remove the muslin bag.

3   Spoon the chutney into jars, cover and seal.

450g (1lb) rhubarb, trimmed, washed and chopped
grated zest and juice of 1 orange
225g (8oz) onions, skinned and chopped
450ml (16fl oz) malt vinegar
400g (14oz) demerara sugar
225g (8oz) raisins
½ level tsp whole allspice berries
1½ level tsp black or white mustard seeds
1½ level tsp black peppercorns

PREPARATION TIME: 20 minutes
COOKING TIME: about 1 hour
MAKES: about 1.1kg (2½lb)
PER SERVING: 50 cals, trace amounts of fat, 13g carbohydrate

Fresh coriander chutney

1   Put all the ingredients in a blender or food processor and blend until smooth.

2   Transfer to a glass or plastic bowl, cover and chill in the refrigerator. It will keep for up to 1 week.

100g (4oz) fresh coriander, washed and dried
1 medium onion, skinned and roughly chopped
2 fresh green chillies, seeded
2.5cm (1 in) piece of fresh root ginger, peeled
1 level tsp salt
2tbsp lemon or lime juice
1 level tbsp desiccated coconut

PREPARATION TIME: 10 minutes
MAKES: 275g (10oz)
PER SERVING: 15 cals, 1g fat, 2g carbohydrate

Hot mango chutney

1   Put all the ingredients, except the sugars, in a preserving pan or large, heavy-based saucepan. Bring to the boil and simmer gently for about 10 minutes or until the fruit is beginning to soften.

2   Add the sugars and heat gently, stirring, until the sugar has dissolved, then bring to the boil. Reduce the heat and simmer, uncovered, for about 45 minutes, stirring occasionally, until thick.

3   Cool the chutney slightly, then spoon into jars, cover and seal.

1.1kg (2½ lb) firm mangoes, just starting to ripen (about 2 large mangoes), peeled, stoned and cut into 2.5cm (1in) pieces
25g (1oz) piece of fresh root ginger, peeled and finely chopped
2–3 small red or green chillies, seeded and chopped
175g (6oz) onion, skinned and roughly chopped
1 garlic clove, skinned and roughly chopped
450g (1lb) cooking apples, peeled, cored and roughly chopped
1 level tsp salt
600ml (1 pint) white wine vinegar
½ level tsp ground cinnamon
225g (8oz) demerara sugar
225g (8oz) granulated sugar

PREPARATION TIME: 20 minutes
COOKING TIME: 1 hour
MAKES: 1.4kg (3lb)
PER SERVING: 40 cals, trace amounts of fat, 11g carbohydrate

Fresh mango chutney

1   Slice the mango in half lengthways through to the stone. Cut all the way round, then, keeping the flat side of the knife against the stone, saw the mango flesh free from the stone. Repeat with the other side.

2   Using the point of a knife, make 5 or 6 diagonal cuts through the flesh, but not through the skin. Then make another 5 or 6 cuts at right angles to the first set, so that you have a diamond pattern in the flesh.

3   Turn the skin inside out so that the cubes of flesh stand up, then cut these off with the knife and place in a bowl.

4   Cut the chilli into fine rings and mix with the mango cubes, lime juice, cayenne pepper and salt. Chill for 1 hour before serving. This chutney will keep for up to 2 days in the refrigerator.

1 large ripe mango
1 fresh green chilli, seeded
juice of 1 lime
¼ level tsp cayenne pepper
½ level tsp salt

PREPARATION TIME: 20 minutes, plus chilling
MAKES: 225g (8oz)
PER SERVING: 25 cals, 0g fat, 6g carbohydrate

Pear and lemon chutney

1   Put the pears, onions, raisins, ginger, lemon rind and juice, sugar, salt and vinegar in a preserving pan. Tie the garlic, chillies and cloves in a piece of muslin and add to the pan.

2   Bring to the boil, then reduce the heat and simmer gently, uncovered, for about 2 hours, stirring occasionally, until the mixture is thick and no excess liquid remains. Remove the muslin bag.

3   Spoon the chutney into jars, cover and seal. Store for 2–3 months before eating.

1.8kg (4lb) pears, peeled, cored and chopped
450g (1lb) onions, skinned and chopped
350g (12oz) seedless raisins, chopped
50g (2oz) stem ginger, chopped
grated rind and juice of 2 lemons
225g (8oz) light brown soft sugar
2 level tbsp salt
1.1 litres (2 pints) distilled vinegar
2 garlic cloves, skinned and crushed
6 dried chillies, crushed
4 whole cloves

PREPARATION TIME: 25 minutes
COOKING TIME: 2 hours
MAKES: 1.8kg (4lb)
PER SERVING: 35 cals, 0g fat, 10g carbohydrate

Mustard relish

1 Put all the vegetables in a large bowl. Dissolve the salt in 1.1 litres (2 pints) water and pour over the vegetables. Cover and leave to stand overnight.

2 Drain the vegetables and rinse well. Blend the mustard seeds, sugar, flour, mustard powder and turmeric together in a large, heavy-based saucepan, then gradually stir in the vinegar. Bring to the boil, stirring.

3 Add the vegetables and simmer, uncovered, for 30 minutes. Stir gently from time to time to prevent sticking.

4 Spoon the relish into jars, cover and seal.

175g (6oz) cucumber, washed and finely chopped

175g (6oz) onion, skinned and finely chopped

225g (8oz) cauliflower, washed and broken into florets

100g (4oz) tomatoes, roughly chopped

1 medium green pepper, washed, seeded and finely chopped

1 medium red pepper, washed, seeded and finely chopped

225g (8oz) fresh gherkins, thickly sliced

25g (1oz) salt

1 level tbsp mustard seeds

250g (9oz) sugar

25g (1oz) plain flour

½ level tsp mustard powder

½ level tsp ground turmeric

450ml (¾ pint) malt vinegar

PREPARATION TIME: 25 minutes, plus standing

COOKING TIME: 40 minutes

MAKES: 1.4kg (3lb)

PER SERVING: 25 cals, trace amounts of fat, 6g carbohydrate

Chunky vegetable relish

1   Cut the carrots into 5 mm (¼ in) dice and blanch in salted boiling water for 4 minutes, then drain well. (The carrot will not tenderize sufficiently if only cooked in the vinegar.)

2   Put all the ingredients in a preserving pan or large, heavy-based saucepan and heat slowly, stirring, until the sugar has dissolved.

3   Boil gently, uncovered, for about 40–50 minutes, stirring occasionally, until the vegetables are just tender and the contents of the pan well reduced. If the mixture starts to become too dry add 4 tbsps of water and continue cooking.

4   Spoon the relish into clean, dry warmed jars, cover and seal.

225g (8oz) carrots, peeled
225g (8oz) swede, peeled and diced
225g (8oz) onion, skinned and chopped
450g (1lb) cooking apples, peeled, cored and roughly chopped
225g (8oz) small cauliflower florets
100g (4oz) sultanas
2 tbsp molasses
3 level tbsp tomato purée
2 tbsp lemon juice
1 garlic clove, skinned and crushed
175g (6oz) dark brown soft sugar
600ml (1 pint) malt vinegar
salt and pepper
½ level tsp ground allspice

PREPARATION TIME: 25 minutes
COOKING TIME: 1 hour
MAKES: 1.4kg (3lb)
PER SERVING: 25 cals, trace amounts of fat, 6g carbohydrate

Tomato relish

1 Layer the tomatoes and cucumber (or marrow) in a bowl, sprinkling each layer with salt. Cover and leave overnight.

2 Next day, drain and rinse well and place in a preserving pan or large, heavy-based saucepan. Add the garlic and pepper.

3 Blend the vinegar with the dry ingredients. Stir into the pan and bring slowly to the boil. Boil gently, uncovered, for about 1 hour, stirring occasionally, until the mixture is soft.

4 Spoon the relish into jars, cover and seal. Store for 3–4 months before use.

1.4kg (3lb) tomatoes, skinned and sliced

450g (1lb) cucumber or marrow, peeled, seeded and roughly chopped

50g (2oz) salt

2 garlic cloves, skinned and finely chopped

1 large red pepper, washed, seeded and roughly chopped

450ml (¾ pint) malt vinegar

1 level tbsp mustard powder

½ level tsp ground allspice

½ level tsp mustard seeds

PREPARATION TIME: 25 minutes, plus standing
COOKING TIME: about 1 hour
MAKES: about 1.8kg (4lb)
PER SERVING: 5 cals, trace amounts of fat, 1g carbohydrate

Sweetcorn relish

1 Cook the corn cobs in boiling salted water for 3 minutes, then drain. Using a sharp knife, cut the corn from the cobs. Coarsely mince the cabbage, onions and red peppers and combine with the corn.

2 Blend the salt, flour, turmeric, sugar and mustard together in a preserving pan then gradually stir in the vinegar. Heat gently, stirring, until the sugar has dissolved, then bring to the boil. Reduce the heat, add the vegetables, and simmer for 25–30 minutes, stirring occasionally.

3 Spoon the relish into jars, cover and seal.

6 corn cobs, trimmed and leaves and silk removed

½ a small white cabbage, trimmed and roughly chopped

2 medium onions, skinned and halved

1½ red peppers, washed, seeded and quartered

2 level tsp salt

2 level tbsp flour

½ level tsp ground turmeric

175g (6oz) sugar

2 level tsp mustard powder

600ml (1 pint) distilled vinegar

PREPARATION TIME: 25 minutes
COOKING TIME: 40 minutes
MAKES: 2.3kg (5lb)
PER SERVING: 20 cals, trace amounts of fat, 4g carbohydrate

Microwave apple chutney

1   Put all the ingredients in a large, heatproof bowl and microwave on HIGH for 5 minutes, stirring occasionally, or until the sugar has dissolved.

2   Microwave on HIGH for about 20 minutes or until the mixture is thick and has no excess liquid. Stir every 5 minutes during cooking to prevent the surface drying out.

3   Pot and cover the chutney. Store for 3 months before eating.

450g (1lb) cooking apples, peeled, cored and finely diced
450g (1lb) onions, skinned and finely chopped
100g (4oz) sultanas
100g (4oz) seedless raisins
150g (5oz) demerara sugar
200ml (7fl oz) malt vinegar
1 level tsp ground ginger
1 level tsp ground cloves
1 level tsp ground allspice
grated rind and juice of ½ lemon

PREPARATION TIME: 20 minutes
COOKING TIME: 25 minutes
MAKES: 900g (2lb)
PER SERVING: 40 cals, trace amounts of fat, 10g carbohydrate

Microwave tomato chutney

1   Put the tomatoes in a large heatproof bowl and just cover with boiling water. Microwave on HIGH for 4 minutes, then lift the tomatoes out one by one, using a slotted spoon, and remove their skins.

2   Put the apples and onion in a blender or food processor and blend to form a thick paste. Coarsely chop the tomatoes.

3   Mix all the ingredients together in a large heatproof bowl. Microwave on HIGH for 35–40 minutes or until the mixture is thick and has no excess liquid. Stir every 5 minutes during cooking and take particular care, stirring more frequently, during the last 5 minutes.

4   Pot and cover the chutney. Store for at least 2 months before eating.

700g (1½ lb) firm tomatoes
225g (8oz) cooking apples, peeled, cored and chopped
1 medium onion, skinned and chopped
100g (4oz) dark brown soft sugar
100g (4oz) sultanas
1 level tsp salt
200ml (7fl oz) malt vinegar
15g (½ oz) ground ginger
½ level tsp cayenne pepper
½ level tsp mustard powder

PREPARATION TIME: 20 minutes
COOKING TIME: 45 minutes
MAKES: 900g (2lb)
PER SERVING: 20 cals, trace amounts of fat, 6g carbohydrate

Pickles

Fruit and vegetable pickles, traditionally made in bulk to preserve fresh summer produce through the winter, can equally well be made in smaller quantities. While pickled onions and piccalilli are well-known favourites, pickled fruits like figs and peaches are equally good and make delicious accompaniments to smoked fish and cold meats, or can be chopped and scattered over salads. Like chutneys, most pickles are best stored for a couple of months before use to allow the flavours to mature, although red cabbage should only be stored for three weeks as it looses its crispness. When making pickles that are dry brined it's essential to rinse off the salt thoroughly before completing the recipe or it will ruin the finished product. Most pickles will keep well for up to a year in a cool, dry place.

Piccalilli

1   Seed the marrow. Finely dice the marrow and cucumber. Top, tail and slice the beans, skin and halve the onions and break the cauliflower into small florets. Layer the vegetables in a large bowl, sprinkling each layer with salt. Add 1.7 litres (3 pints) water, cover and leave for 24 hours in a cool place.

2   The next day, remove the vegetables and rinse and drain them well. Blend the sugar, mustard, ginger and garlic with 450ml (¾ pint) of the vinegar in a large pan. Heat to dissolve the sugar.

3   Add the vegetables, bring to the boil and simmer for 20 minutes or until the vegetables are cooked but still crisp.

4   Blend the flour and turmeric with the remaining vinegar and stir into the cooked vegetables. Bring to the boil and cook for 2 minutes.

5   Spoon the pickle into jars, cover and seal.

1.4kg (3lb) mixed marrow, cucumber, beans, small onions and cauliflower (prepared weight – see method)

175g (6oz) salt

125g (4½ oz) sugar

1½ level tsp mustard powder

1 level tsp ground ginger

1 garlic clove, skinned and crushed

600ml (1 pint) distilled vinegar

25g (1oz) plain flour

1 level tbsp ground turmeric

PREPARATION TIME: 30 minutes, plus standing
COOKING TIME: 25 minutes
MAKES: 1.5kg (3¼lb)
PER SERVING: 15 cals, trace amounts of fat, 3g carbohydrate

Sweet green tomato pickle

1   Place the vinegar, sugar and cinnamon in a large saucepan with 150ml (¼ pint) water. Heat gently, stirring, until the sugar has dissolved, then bring to the boil.

2   Add the tomatoes and continue cooking for 5 minutes. Pour into a bowl, cover and leave for 1 week.

3   Strain the vinegar into a large saucepan and boil for 10 minutes. Add the tomatoes and boil for a further 5 minutes. Pack into jars, cover and seal.

300ml (½ pint) malt vinegar

900g (2lb) sugar

1 level tsp ground cinnamon

1.4kg (3lb) small green tomatoes, skinned

PREPARATION TIME: 20 minutes, plus standing
COOKING TIME: 25 minutes
MAKES: 1.4kg (3lb)
PER SERVING: 65 cals, trace amounts of fat, 18g carbohydrate

Pickled onions

1   Place the unskinned onions in a large bowl. Dissolve half the salt in 2.3 litres (4 pints) water, pour over the onions and leave for 12 hours.

2   Drain and skin the onions, then cover with fresh brine, made with the remaining salt and a further 2.3 litres (4 pints) water. Leave for 24–36 hours.

3   Drain the onions and rinse well and pack them into jars. Cover with the spiced vinegar. Cover and seal the jars and leave for 3 months before use.

1.8kg (4lb) pickling onions
450g (1lb) salt
1.1 litres (2 pints) spiced vinegar
  (see page 116)

PREPARATION TIME: 25 minutes, plus standing;
MAKES: 1.8kg (4lb)
PER SERVING: 10 cals, trace amounts of fat, 2g carbohydrate

Sweet and sour figs

1   Put the vinegar in a large, shallow pan with the ginger, allspice, peppercorns, cloves, cinnamon, lemon rind, honey and sugar. Heat gently, stirring, until the sugar has dissolved.

2   Bring to the boil, boil for 1 minute, then remove from the heat. Wipe the figs, trim off any long stalks and discard. Thickly slice the figs into the warm vinegar. Bring to the boil, then simmer, uncovered, for 1 minute, gently pushing the fig slices under the vinegar. Carefully transfer the figs and vinegar to a large non-metallic bowl. Cover tightly with cling film and leave overnight.

3   Remove the fig slices from the vinegar with a slotted spoon. Tightly pack into clean, preheated jars. Return the vinegar mixture to a clean saucepan and bring to the boil. Boil rapidly until reduced to 150ml (¼ pint).

4   Pour the hot vinegar into the jars. Cover and seal. Store for at least 1 week before using.

450ml (16fl oz) distilled malt
  vinegar
small piece of fresh root ginger,
  peeled and thinly sliced
3 allspice berries
6 black peppercorns
3 whole cloves
2 cinnamon sticks
pared rind of 1 lemon
2 level tbsp honey
250g (9oz) sugar
700g (1½ lb) firm, green figs

PREPARATION TIME: 20 minutes, plus standing
COOKING TIME: 15 minutes
MAKES: about 700g (1½lb)
PER SERVING: 135 cals, 0g fat, 35g carbohydrate (serves 10, including syrup)

Lemon pickle

1 Cut the fruit (with the skin) into small pieces, remove any pips and catch any juice in a bowl. Mix the fruit pieces and juice with the salt, turmeric, chilli powder and garam masala.

2 Pack the fruit into a large sterile screw-topped jar and keep in a warm cupboard or, when possible, in the hot sun, for a week, giving it a good shake each day.

3 The pickle is ready when the skins are tender. Store well covered.

Note:
Garam masala is a flavouring made by mixing 1 level tsp each of ground cloves, ground cinnamon, freshly ground black pepper, ground cumin seeds and ground cardamom seeds.

Variation: sweet lemon pickle
Add 75g (3oz) demerara sugar to the ingredients above to give a sweet pickle. A few chillies may be added to make it hotter.

Variation: lime pickle
Substitute limes for the lemons in the recipe above.

450g (1lb) ripe, juicy lemons, washed
3 level tbsp salt
1 level tsp ground turmeric
1½ level tsp chilli powder
2 level tsp garam masala

PREPARATION TIME: 20 minutes, plus standing
MAKES: about 450g (1lb)
PER SERVING: 5 cals, 0g fat, 1g carbohydrate

Spiced pickled peaches

1   Push two cloves into each peach half. Place the sugar, vinegar, lemon rind and cinnamon in a saucepan and heat gently, stirring, for about 5 minutes or until the sugar has dissolved. Add the peach halves to the pan and simmer the fruit in the sweetened vinegar until soft.

2   Drain the fruit and pack into jars. Continue boiling the vinegar until it is slightly reduced and beginning to thicken. Strain the vinegar syrup and pour sufficient over the fruit to cover.

3   Cover and seal the jars. Store for 2–3 months before use.

about 30 whole cloves
900g (2lb) peaches, skinned, stoned
    and halved
450g (1lb) sugar
300ml (½ pint) white wine vinegar
thinly pared rind of ½ a lemon
1 small cinnamon stick

PREPARATION TIME: 15 minutes
COOKING TIME: about 15 minutes
PER SERVING: 350 cals, 0g fat, 91g
carbohydrate (serves 6)

Pickled plums

1   Place all the ingredients, except the plums, in a large, heavy-based saucepan. Heat gently, stirring, until the sugar has dissolved. Bring to the boil, then remove from the heat. Leave until cold, then strain, return to the pan and bring to the boil again.

2   Prick the plums with a needle, put them in a deep bowl, pour the spiced vinegar over, cover and leave for 5 days.

3   Strain the vinegar from the plums into a saucepan, bring to the boil and pour over the fruit again. Cover and leave for another 5 days.

4   Strain the vinegar from the plums into a saucepan and bring to the boil again. Pack the plums into jars, pour the boiling vinegar over, cover and seal.

450g (1lb) sugar
thinly pared rind of ½ a lemon
2 whole cloves
small piece of fresh root ginger
300ml (½ pint) malt vinegar
900g (2lb) plums

PREPARATION TIME: 15 minutes,
plus standing
COOKING TIME: about 10 minutes
PER SERVING: 260 cals, 0g fat, 69g
carbohydrate (serves 8)

Mixed dill pickle

1 Wash the cauliflower and divide into small florets; wash and slice the courgettes into 5mm (¼ inch) diagonal pieces; wash and seed the pepper and cut into 5mm (¼ inch) strips; wash, top and tail the beans and cut in half; skin the onions, leaving the roots intact; split the cucumber in half lengthways, then slice thickly.

2 Place all the prepared vegetables in a large bowl. Cover with the coarse salt. Mix, cover and leave in a cold place for 24 hours.

3 Place the remaining ingredients in a preserving pan. Heat gently to simmering point. Remove from the heat and leave to cool completely.

4 Drain the vegetables, rinse well and drain again. Bring two large pans of water to the boil. Add the vegetables and bring back to the boil. Drain the vegetables and refresh under cold water to stop the cooking process and preserve the colour. Allow to drain well.

5 Pack the vegetables into preheated jars. Leave to stand for 1 hour, then drain off the excess liquid. Pour over the cooled pickling vinegar to cover completely. Cover and seal the jars. The pickle will darken a little on storing but it will remain clear if stored in the refrigerator.

1 cauliflower (about 550g/1¼ lb), trimmed
175g (6oz) courgettes
1 green pepper (about 225g/8oz)
175g (6oz) fine green beans
100g (4oz) pickling or button onions
1 cucumber
225g (8oz) coarse salt
1.1–1.3 litres (2–2¼ pints) white wine vinegar
2 level tbsp pickling spice
1 level tbsp salt
100g (4oz) sugar
2 garlic cloves, skinned
2 good stalks of fresh dill
1 level tsp dried dill
2 stalks of tarragon

PREPARATION TIME: 30 minutes, plus standing
COOKING TIME: 15 minutes
PER SERVING: 14 cals, trace amounts of fat, 1g carbohydrate (1tbsp without liquid)

Microwave Indonesian vegetable pickle

1   Put the ginger, garlic, turmeric and oil in a large heatproof bowl and microwave on HIGH for 2 minutes, stirring occasionally. Add the vinegar and microwave on HIGH for 3–5 minutes or until boiling.

2   Meanwhile, cut the cucumber and carrots into 5 mm (¼ inch) slices, and break the cauliflower into tiny florets.

3   Add the vegetables to the boiling vinegar, cover and microwave on HIGH for 2 minutes or until the liquid just returns to the boil. When boiling, microwave for a further 2 minutes. Stir in the remaining ingredients and mix thoroughly together.

4   Pour into jars, cover and seal.

1cm (½ inch) piece of fresh root
    ginger, peeled and grated
2 large garlic cloves, skinned and
    crushed
2 level tsp ground turmeric
45ml (3tbsp) vegetable oil
150ml (¼ pint) spiced pickling
    vinegar (see page 116)
½ cucumber
2 large carrots
175g (6oz) cauliflower florets
1–2 green chillies, seeded and sliced
4 level tbsp sesame seeds
100g (4oz) dark brown soft sugar
100g (4oz) salted peanuts, roughly
    chopped

PREPARATION TIME: 20 minutes
COOKING TIME: 11 minutes
MAKES: 700 kg (1½ lb)
PER SERVING: 65 cals, 4g fat, 5g
carbohydrate

Pickled red cabbage

1   Layer the cabbage and onions in a large bowl, sprinkling each layer with salt, then cover and leave overnight.

2   The next day, drain the cabbage and onions thoroughly, rinse off the salt and pack into jars.

3   Pour the spiced vinegar into a saucepan and heat gently. Add the sugar and stir until dissolved. Leave to cool, then pour over the cabbage and onion. Cover and seal the jars. Use within 2–3 weeks as the cabbage tends to lose its crispness.

about 1.4kg (3lb) firm, red cabbage,
    finely shredded
2 large onions, skinned and sliced
4 level tbsp salt
2.3 litres (4 pints) spiced vinegar
    (see page 116)
1 level tbsp dark brown soft sugar

PREPARATION TIME: 20 minutes,
plus standing
COOKING TIME: 5 minutes
MAKES: 1.4kg (3lb)
PER SERVING: 5 cals, trace amounts
of fat, 1g carbohydrate

Sauces, spreads, oils and vinegars

This chapter contains an assortment of long- and short-term preserves, made using various techniques. Some are straightforward infusions of herbs and spices in oils and vinegars for cooking and dressings, while others rely on traditional preserve-making ingredients and techniques. Homemade, bottled sauces and ketchups use similar ingredients to chutney, such as fruit, vegetables, vinegar, spices and sugar, but are sieved after cooking to give a smooth consistency for pouring or spooning. Vinegar is the main preservative, but sauces may be sterilized once bottled to prolong storage life for several months, (see page 19). 'Short-term' preserves like pesto and tapenade can be stored for up to a week or two, making an instant meal when tossed with fresh pasta or spread on toast for lunchtime snacks. All the recipes make fairly small quantities but can easily be doubled up if you've got a glut of ingredients.

Sweet and sour cranberry sauce

1   Tie the cinnamon, allspice and cloves in a piece of muslin and put in a saucepan with the apples, ginger, cranberries and vinegar. Bring to the boil, cover and simmer for 10 minutes or until the fruit is soft but still retains its shape.

2   Remove the pan from the heat and stir in the sugar. Return to the heat and simmer gently, uncovered, stirring continuously, for a further 20 minutes. Remove the spices.

3   Transfer the sauce to jars and cover with vinegar-proof lids. Store in a cool, dry place for up to 3 months.

2 cinnamon sticks

6 whole allspice berries

6 cloves

225g (8oz) cooking apples, peeled, cored and chopped

1cm (½in) piece of fresh root ginger, peeled and finely chopped, or 1 level tsp ground ginger

450g (1lb) cranberries

300ml (½ pint) cider vinegar

350g (12oz) demerara sugar

PREPARATION TIME: 15 minutes
COOKING TIME: 30 minutes
MAKES: 900g (2lb)
PER SERVING: 40 cals, 0g fat, 11g carbohydrate

Mint sauce

1   Put the chopped mint into dry, wide-necked jars. Dissolve the sugar in the vinegar in a medium-sized saucepan, stirring with a wooden spoon, and bring to the boil. Leave until cold. Pour over the mint and seal to make the jars airtight. Store in the fridge for up to five days.

2   To serve, lift out sufficient mint with a wooden spoon, together with a little of the liquid. Put into a jug or sauceboat and add a little fresh vinegar. Store in the refrigerator for 4–5 days.

100g (4oz) fresh mint, washed, dried and finely chopped

225g (8oz) sugar

300ml (½ pint) vinegar

PREPARATION TIME: 5 minutes, plus cooling
COOKING TIME: 3 minutes
MAKES: 300ml (½ pint)
PER SERVING: 75 cals, 0g fat, 20g carbohydrate

Apple sauce

1 Put all the ingredients in a medium, heavy-based saucepan with 150ml (¼ pint) water. Cover and cook gently for about 15 minutes until the apples are soft and pulpy, stirring occasionally to prevent sticking.

2 Press the pulp through a sieve for a smooth sauce, or beat well for a more textured one.

3 Spoon into small, thoroughly clean, dry jars, seal and sterilize.

900g (2lb) cooking apples, peeled, cored and cut into chunks
finely grated rind and juice of 1 lemon
8 whole cloves
50g (2oz) caster sugar

PREPARATION TIME: 15 minutes
COOKING TIME: 15 minutes
MAKES: 700g (1½lb)
PER SERVING: 20 cals, 0g fat, 5g carbohydrate

Cranberry and red onion marmalade

1 Heat the oil in a medium-sized pan and fry the onions gently for 5 minutes.

2 Add the orange juice, pickling spice, sugar and port. Simmer gently for 40 minutes.

3 Add the cranberries and cook for 20 minutes. Cool and chill for up to 7 days, or freeze for up to 1 month.

2 tbsp olive oil
500g (1lb 2 oz) red onions, sliced
Juice of 1 orange
1 level tbsp pickling spice
150g (5oz) dark muscovado sugar
150ml (¼ pint) ruby port
450g (1lb) cranberries

PREPARATION TIME: 30 minutes
COOKING TIME: 1 hour 5 minutes
MAKES: 900g (2lb)
PER SERVING: 35 cals, 1g fat, 7g carbohydrate

Wholegrain mustard with honey

1 Place the mustard seeds and spices in a medium heavy-based saucepan. Heat gently for 1 minute, stirring the seeds and spices.

2 Add the vinegar and 4 tablespoons of boiling water. Bring to just below boiling then pour into a bowl, cover and leave to soak overnight.

3 Place the mixture in a food processor with the salt and honey and blend until smooth.

4 Place in sterilized jars and seal with vinegar-proof lids or cling wrap. Keep chilled for 1 week to improve flavour. Store in the fridge for up to 1 month.

125g (4½oz) white mustard seeds
150ml (¼ pint) garlic white wine vinegar
1 level tbsp ground cinnamon
½ level tsp of ground ginger
3tbsp clear honey
½ tsp salt

PREPARATION TIME: 15 minutes, plus standing
MAKES: 200g (7oz)
PER SERVING: 40 cals, 3g fat, 2g carbohydrate

The ultimate barbeque sauce

1 Mix together the oil, garlic, vinegar, sherry, tomato paste and chilli sauce.

2 Turn into a small saucepan and add the passata and honey. Bring to the boil, reduce the heat and simmer gently for 10–15 minutes until thickened and glossy.

Note
Quick to make, this sauce goes well with chicken, pork, burgers or pork sausages.

3 tbsp olive oil
3 garlic cloves, finely chopped
3 tbsp balsamic vinegar
4 tbsp dry sherry
3 level tbsp sundried tomato paste or tomato puree
3tbsp sweet chilli sauce
300ml (½ pint) passata
5 tbsp runny honey

PREPARATION TIME: 5 minutes;
COOKING TIME: 15 minutes
MAKES: about 300ml (½ pint)
PER SERVING: 60 cals, 3g fat, 6g carbohydrate

Spicy brown sauce

1 Peel, core and roughly chop the apples and put in a preserving pan or large heavy-based saucepan with the remaining ingredients. Simmer until the sugar has dissolved, then bring to the boil, reduce the heat and simmer gently for 45 minutes, stirring frequently until thickened and pulpy. If the mixture becomes too dry add 4 tbsp water and continue cooking.

2 Cool, then blend the mixture in a food processor or blender, in batches, until smooth. Press through a sieve to make a smooth sauce and transfer to a jug.

3 Pour the hot sauce into clean, dry warm bottles, seal and sterilize.

750g (1½ lb) cooking apples
250g (8oz) onions, skinned and roughly chopped
1 hot green chilli, deseeded and finely chopped
1 garlic clove, chopped
2 level tsp paprika
15g (½ oz) fresh root ginger, peeled and grated
100g (3½ oz) sultanas
250ml (8fl oz) red wine vinegar
2 level tsp salt
250g (8oz) light muscovado sugar

PREPARATION TIME: 20 minutes
COOKING TIME: about 45 minutes
MAKES: about 550ml (1 pint)
PER SERVING: 80 cals, trace amounts of fat, 21g carbohydrate

Tomato ketchup

1 Put the tomatoes in a pan and cook over a very low heat until they pulp. Bring to the boil and boil rapidly, stirring frequently, until the pulp thickens.

2 Press through a nylon sieve and return to the pan. Add the remaining ingredients. Simmer until the mixture thickens. Pour the hot ketchup into warm bottles, seal and sterilize.

2.7kg (6lb) ripe tomatoes, sliced
225g (8oz) sugar
300ml (½ pint) spiced vinegar (see page 116)
1 tbsp tarragon vinegar (optional)
pinch of cayenne
1 level tsp ground paprika
1 level tsp salt

PREPARATION TIME: 20 minutes
COOKING TIME: 20 minutes
MAKES: about 1.1 litres (2 pints)
PER SERVING: 30 cals, trace amounts of fat, 7g carbohydrate

Apricot and cardamom spread

1   Crush the cardamom pods in a pestle and mortar (or in a strong bowl with the end of a rolling pin) until the pods break open. There is no need to crush them finely.

2   Make up the lemon juice to 300ml (½ pint) with cold water. Put the liquid, crushed cardamoms and ground cardamom in a heavy-based saucepan and cook until just boiling. Remove from the heat and leave for 30 minutes to infuse.

3   Strain the liquid and return to the pan with the apricots. Bring to the boil, cover, lower the heat and simmer very gently for 20–25 minutes or until thick, stirring occasionally to prevent sticking. Add a little more water if necessary.

4   Mash the fruit with a fork or process in a food processor until smooth. Spoon into jars. Cover and seal. Store in the fridge for up to 1 month.

15ml (1tbsp) green cardamom pods
juice of 1 lemon
1 level tsp ground cardamom
500g (1lb 2oz) no-soak dried
   apricots, chopped

PREPARATION TIME: 15 minutes, plus standing
COOKING TIME: 30 minutes
MAKES: 700g (1lb 8oz)
PER SERVING: 30 cals, 0g fat, 6g carbohydrate

Anchovy caper spread

1   Drain the anchovies, reserving the oil. Put the anchovies in a food processor with the capers, olives, mustard, basil, thyme and pepper.

2   Blend until smooth, then add the oil from the anchovies, and process again until reduced to a soft paste.

3   Pack the spread into small attractive pots or jars, cover with a layer of olive oil and seal tightly. Store in the fridge for several weeks.

2 tins anchovy fillets
1 level tbsp capers
25g (1oz) stoned black olives
1 level tbsp coarse-grained mustard
pinch of dried basil and thyme
freshly ground pepper
30–45 ml (2–3 tbsp) olive oil

PREPARATION TIME: 20 minutes
MAKES: 90–120ml (6–8tbsp)
PER SERVING: 80 cals, 9g fat, trace carbohydrate (per level tbsp)

Plum and apple spread

1 Put the plums and apples in a preserving pan or a large, heavy-based saucepan with the grape juice and 300ml (½ pint) cold water.

2 Bring slowly to the boil, then simmer over a low heat for about 50 minutes or until the fruit is reduced to a very thick purée. Stir frequently, pressing the fruit into the liquid with a wooden spoon so that it breaks up and becomes pulpy. Towards the end of cooking, add the cinnamon and stir continuously to ensure that the purée does not stick to the bottom of the pan.

3 Remove the pan from the heat and leave for about 5 minutes or until the mixture has settled. Spoon the hot spread into jars and leave until completely cold. Cover and seal. Store in the fridge for up to 3 weeks.

900g (2lb) ripe plums, such as
   Victoria, halved and stoned
900g (2lb) eating apples, quartered
   and cored
600ml (1 pint) unsweetened red
   grape juice
½ level tsp ground cinnamon

PREPARATION TIME: 15 minutes,
plus standing
COOKING TIME: 1 hour
MAKES: 900g (2lb)
PER SERVING: 25 cals, 0g fat, 6g
carbohydrate

Drambuie butter

1 Put the butter and sugar in a food processor and blend until soft and pale. Add the grated orange rind, the mixed spice and cardamom. Process until soft and well creamed, then gradually drip in the Drambuie and a good squeeze of lemon juice.

2 Pack the butter into pots, cover and store in the fridge for up to a week.

Variation
Use brandy or whisky instead of the Drambuie.

100g (4oz) butter, softened
100g (4oz) light brown soft sugar
grated rind of ¼ orange
¼ level tsp ground mixed spice
pinch of ground green cardamom
45–60ml (3–4 tbsp) Drambuie
squeeze of lemon juice

PREPARATION TIME: 10 minutes
MAKES: 225g (8oz)
PER SERVING: 140 cals, 9g fat, 12g
carbohydrate

Tapenade

1 Soak the anchovies overnight in a little milk. Drain well.

2 Place the anchovies, olives, capers and tuna fish in a blender or food processor and blend to a thick paste.

3 Gradually add the olive oil and juice drop by drop, as if making mayonnaise, to form a smooth paste. Add the brandy and black pepper to taste.

4 Pack into small attractive pots or jars, cover with a layer of olive oil and seal tightly. The mixture will keep in the fridge for several weeks.

5 To serve, stir in the top layer of oil and serve spread over hot bread or toast, pasta or recipe of your choice.

50g (2oz) can anchovy fillets
milk
75g (3oz) stoned black olives
    (about 36)
4 level tbsp capers
100g (4oz) can tuna in oil, drained
50ml (2fl oz) olive oil
15ml (1tbsp) lemon juice
about 15ml (1tbsp) brandy
black pepper

PREPARATION TIME: 10 minutes, plus standing; serves 3–4
PER SERVING: 220 cals, 21g fat, 0g carbohydrate (for 4 people)

Hot harissa paste

1 Soak the chillies in hot water for 1 hour. Drain well, then put in a pestle and mortar or electric mill with the garlic clove and spices, and grind to a paste.

2 Put into a small jar, cover with olive oil and seal. Harissa will keep in the fridge for up to 2 months. The oil can be used in salad dressings.

25g (1oz) dried red chillies
1 garlic clove, skinned and chopped
1 level tsp caraway seeds
1 level tsp cumin seeds
1 level tsp coriander seeds
pinch of salt
olive oil

PREPARATION TIME: 10 minutes, plus standing
MAKES: 45ml (3tbsp)
PER SERVING: 15 cals, 3g fat, 0g carbohydrate

Yogurt cheeses in oil

1   Spoon the yogurt in a mound on to a large piece of muslin. Gather the ends of the muslin up around the yogurt and tie in a bundle with string. Hang up the yogurt over a bowl to catch the drips and leave in a cool place to drain for 24 hours.

2   Pour the olive oil into a sterile jar until it is about 2.5cm (1 inch) deep. Unwrap the yogurt cheese and roll into small balls. Drop the cheeses, one by one, into the oil, adding more oil each time you add a cheese so they do not stick together.

3   Pour in enough oil to cover the cheeses completely. Add the herbs and chillies and garlic, if using. Cover and leave for at least 3 days. Store in a cool place for up to 2 weeks. Serve the cheese with salads, warm breads or baked potatoes. The oil can be used to flavour salads or for sautéing vegetables.

600ml (1 pint) Greek yogurt
olive oil
sprigs of fresh herbs, such as bay
    leaves, coriander, thyme and
    rosemary
chillies (optional)
garlic cloves, skinned (optional)

PREPARATION TIME: 25 minutes, plus standing
MAKES: about 16 cheeses
PER SERVING: 40 cals, 3g fat, trace amounts of carbohydrate

Herb and garlic oil

1   Place all the ingredients in a glass jar or bottle with a tight-fitting lid. Seal and then shake well to mix.

2   Leave in a cool, dry place for 2 weeks before using. Store for up to 3 months.

Variation: herb and saffron oil
Add ½ level tsp crushed saffron strands to the herb and garlic oil.

2 sprigs of fresh rosemary or 2 level
    tsp dried
2 sprigs of fresh tarragon or mint
2 bay leaves
2 garlic cloves, skinned
6 black peppercorns
3 juniper berries
about 1 litre (1¾ pints) olive oil
150ml (¼ pint) walnut oil

PREPARATION TIME: 5 minutes, plus standing
MAKES: 1.1 litres (2 pints)
PER SERVING: 115 cals, 13g fat, 0g carbohydrate (for a 15ml serving)

Goats' cheeses in herb and saffron oil

1   Place the cheeses in a large, wide-necked jar. Gently pour over the herb and saffron oil to cover completely.

2   Cover tightly and store in the fridge for at least 1 week before using. It will keep for up to 1 month. To serve, spread on warm bread with a little of the flavoured oil and brown under a hot grill. The oil can also be used for drizzling over crusty bread or mixed salad leaves, or for basting grilled meats and fish.

8 fresh goats' cheeses (about 50g/2oz each) such as Crottin

1.1 litres (2 pints) herb and saffron oil (see page 111)

PREPARATION TIME: 5 minutes;
MAKES: about 1.6 litres (3 pints)
PER SERVING: 130 cals, 12g fat, trace carbohydrate (per cheese)

Pesto

1   Place the basil, garlic, pine nuts, salt and pepper and olive oil in an electric blender or food processor and blend until very creamy.

2   Transfer the mixture to a bowl, grate in the cheese and mix together thoroughly. Transfer to a jar and cover tightly. Pesto will keep for up to 2 weeks in the fridge. Taste and adjust the seasoning before serving.

50g (2oz) fresh basil leaves
2 garlic cloves, skinned
2 level tbsp pine nuts
salt and freshly ground pepper
100ml (4fl oz) olive oil
50g (2oz) Parmesan cheese

PREPARATION TIME: 10 minutes
MAKES: enough to dress 4 servings of pasta
PER SERVING: 320 cals, 32g fat, 1g carbohydrate (per serving)

Hazelnut and coriander pesto

1   Spread the hazelnuts on a baking sheet and cook under a hot grill until lightly toasted. Tip into a blender or food processor.

2   Trim the stalks from the coriander and discard. Put the leaves into the blender with the garlic and the lemon rind and juice. Process until finely chopped, then, with the machine still running, gradually add the oil in a thin, steady stream until you have a fairly thick, sauce-like consistency.

3   Season with black pepper and a little salt. Turn into a bowl or a jar and cover tightly. Store in the fridge for up to 2 weeks.

75g (3oz) hazelnuts
1 large bunch of coriander, weighing about 100g (4oz)
2–3 garlic cloves, skinned and crushed
finely grated rind and juice of ½ lemon
about 150ml (¼ pint) olive, sunflower or corn oil
salt and freshly ground black pepper

PREPARATION TIME: 10 minutes (enough for 4–6 servings of pasta)
MAKES: 300ml (½ pint)
PER SERVING: 125 cals, 13g fat, trace amounts of carbohydrate

Salsa verde

1   Put all the ingredients in a bowl or screw-topped jar and whisk or shake together.

2   Transfer to a screw-topped jar, if necessary, cover tightly and store in the fridge for 2–3 weeks. Serve with pasta, baked potatoes, fish, grilled meat or salads.

100ml (4 fl oz) olive oil

15ml (1 tbsp) white wine vinegar or lemon juice

3 level tbsp chopped fresh parsley

2 level tbsp capers, chopped

1 garlic clove, skinned and finely chopped

3 anchovy fillets, drained and finely chopped

½ level tsp prepared mustard

freshly ground pepper

PREPARATION TIME: 5 minutes;
MAKES: about 200ml (7fl oz)
PER SERVING: 60 cals, 7g fat, 0g carbohydrate (per level tbsp)

Salsa di noci (walnut dressing)

1   Discard the crusts from the slice of bread and soak it in cold water for a few minutes.

2   Squeeze out the excess moisture and put the bread in a food processor.

3   Add the walnuts, lemon juice, garlic, salt and pepper, and blend until the mixture is very finely ground.

4   Gradually add the oil through the funnel, while the machine is still running, until it is all incorporated. Transfer the dressing to a screw-topped jar and store in the fridge for up to 1 week.

5   Check the seasoning and stir well before serving with salads, baked potatoes, pasta or steamed vegetables.

1 small slice of wholemeal bread

40g (1½ oz) shelled walnuts

10ml (2tsp) lemon juice

1 garlic clove, skinned

salt and freshly ground pepper

200ml (7fl oz) olive oil

PREPARATION TIME: 10 minutes, plus standing
MAKES: 225ml (8fl oz)
PER SERVING: 120 cals, 13g fat, 1g carbohydrate (per tsp)

Spiced vinegar

1   Put the vinegar, spices and bay leaf in a medium saucepan, bring to the boil and pour into a bowl. Cover and leave to marinate for 2 hours.

2   Strain the vinegar through muslin, pour into sterilized bottles and seal with airtight and vinegar-proof tops.

1.1 litres (2 pints) vinegar
2 level tbsp blades of mace
1 level tbsp whole allspice berries
1 level tbsp whole cloves
18cm (7in) cinnamon stick
6 peppercorns
4 dried red chillies
1 small bay leaf

PREPARATION TIME: 10 minutes, plus standing
COOKING TIME: 5 minutes
MAKES: 1.1 litres (2 pints)
PER SERVING: 0 cals, 0g fat, 0g carbohydrate

Horseradish vinegar

1   Peel the horseradish and finely grate the flesh. Put in a thoroughly cleaned 300 ml (½ pint) jar.

2   Bring the vinegar to the boil and pour it over the horseradish. Leave to cool then cover with a vinegar proof lid and store for up to 6 months.

Note
To make horseradish sauce, thoroughly drain 2 to 3 level tablespoons of the horseradish and mix in a bowl with 100ml (3½ fl oz) whipped cream or crème fraiche, 1 to 2 level teaspoons caster sugar and a little salt. Mix well and chill until ready to serve. The strained vinegar can be used in salad dressings and sauces.

40g (1½ oz) fresh horseradish root
300ml (½ pint) white wine vinegar

PREPARATION TIME: 5 minutes
COOKING TIME: 2 minutes
MAKES: about 300ml (½ pint)
PER SERVING: 0 cals, 0g fat, 0g carbohydrate

Fruit vinegar

1   Put the fruit in a bowl and break it up slightly with the back of a wooden spoon. Add the vinegar, cover and leave to stand for 3–4 days, stirring occasionally.

2   Strain the vinegar through muslin and pour over the extra fruits in bottles. Cover with vinegar proof lids and store for 2 weeks before use.

450g (1lb) raspberries, blackberries or blackcurrants, plus a handful extra for bottling

600ml (1 pint) red or white wine vinegar

PREPARATION TIME: 5 minutes, plus standing
MAKES: 600ml (1 pint)
PER SERVING: 0 cals, 0g fat, 0g carbohydrate

Herb vinegar

1   Pour the vinegar over the chosen herb in a medium saucepan. Bring slowly to the boil then turn into a large bowl. Cover and leave to infuse overnight.

2   Strain the vinegar through muslin and pour into a clean bottle. Add a few sprigs of the fresh herb for identification and cover with a vinegar proof lid. Store for 1 week before using.

25g (1oz) fresh tarragon, thyme or rosemary, plus extra sprigs for bottling

600ml (1 pint) white wine vinegar

PREPARATION TIME: 5 minutes, plus standing
MAKES: 600ml (1 pint)
PER SERVING: 0 cals, 0g fat, 0g carbohydrate

Preserved lemons

1   Wash and dry the lemons. Cut 5 of the lemons almost into quarters, keeping then intact at one end. Open them out slightly and sprinkle 1 tbsp of the salt onto the cut flesh of each.

2   Close up the lemons again and pack then as tightly as possible into a thoroughly clean jar, tucking the bay leaves in between them. Squeeze the juice from the remaining lemons and pour into the jar. Top up with cold water to cover the lemons completely, tapping the jar gently to remove any air bubbles. Spoon over a thin layer of olive oil. Store in a cool place for 3 weeks before use.

3   To use, remove the lemons from the jar as required using a wooden spoon. Rinse and cut away the pulp, slicing or chopping the peel into pieces. Small quantities of the tangy juices can be used in dressings and marinades. Preserved lemons will keep for up to 6 months. Here the preserved lemons have been served with couscous garnished with slices of fresh lemon.

8 unwaxed lemons
5 level tbsp coarse sea salt
4 bay leaves
olive oil

PREPARATION TIME: 10 minutes, plus standing
MAKES: 1kg (2¼lb)
PER SERVING: 5 cals, trace amounts of fat, trace amounts of carbohydrate

Mincemeat

Mincemeats were originally made as a way of preserving meats without cooking or brining them. The only remnant of this tradition is the frequent addition of beef suet to a recipe, although today this is often replaced with vegetable suet, or left out altogether. Instead, the focus is on a rich blend of fruits, usually dried, or a mixture of fresh and dried with sugar, alcohol and spices. It's the blend of fruits, combined with the sugar syrup that keeps modern mincemeat moist and juicy. Pot and cover mincemeat as for jam and store it in a cool, dry place for up to three months (see chosen recipe for precise storage times). If during storage it starts oozing syrup, this might be a sign of fermentation. Tip the mixture out into a pan, boil it up, pot into cleaned sterilized jars and store in the fridge. Alternatively, if the surface of the mincemeat dries out, stir in a little brandy, rum or the type of alcohol used in the original recipe.

Quick mincemeat

1   Mix the apples, dried fruit and peel in a large bowl. Add the sugar and mix well together.

2   Add the remaining ingredients, mix well, pot and cover as for jam. Store in a cool place for no more than a week.

Note
This is a quick, fruity mincemeat, not suitable for long keeping, but popular with those who do not like suet.

225g (8oz) cooking apples, peeled, cored and roughly chopped
450g (1lb) seedless raisins and currants, mixed, or 450g (1lb) sultanas
100g (4oz) chopped mixed peel
100g (4oz) demerara sugar
225g (8oz) seedless green grapes, skinned and chopped
grated rind of 1 orange and 1 lemon
15ml (1tbsp) lemon juice
1 level tsp ground cinnamon or mixed spice
a pinch of salt

PREPARATION TIME: 15 minutes
MAKES: 900g (2lb)
PER SERVING: 55 cals, 0g fat, 14g carbohydrate

Almond whisky mincemeat

1　Put the almonds, apricots, figs, dates and apples in a non-metallic bowl with the remaining ingredients except the citrus rind and juice.

2　Stir in the grated rind and strained juice of the oranges and lemon. Cover and leave to stand overnight.

3　Stir well, pack tightly into jars and cover as for jam. Store in a cool, dry place for about 6 weeks before using. (Will store for a further 3 months.)

100g (4oz) blanched almonds, finely chopped
100g (4oz) no-soak dried apricots, finely chopped
50g (2oz) dried figs, finely chopped
50g (2oz) stoned dried dates, finely chopped
350g (12oz) cooking apples, peeled, cored and finely chopped
225g (8oz) sultanas
150g (5oz) seedless raisins
175g (6oz) shredded suet
1 level tsp ground cinnamon
1 level tsp grated nutmeg
pinch of ground allspice
100g (4oz) dark brown soft sugar
300ml (½ pint) whisky
finely grated rind and juice of
　2 oranges
finely grated rind and juice of
　1 small lemon

PREPARATION TIME: 20 minutes, plus standing
MAKES: about 1.1kg (2½lb)
PER SERVING: 100 cals, 5g fat, 11g carbohydrate

Spicy carrot mincemeat

1 Finely grate the apples and carrots.

2 Place in a large bowl and add all the remaining ingredients. Mix well together.

3 Put into jars and cover as for jam. Allow 2 weeks to mature before use.

225g (8oz) cooking apples, peeled and cored
100g (4oz) carrots, peeled
450 g (1lb) sultanas
225g (8oz) currants
grated rind and juice of 1 orange
100g (4oz) shredded suet
pinch of salt
100g (4oz) demerara sugar
60ml (4tbsp) sherry
1 level tsp grated nutmeg
1 level tsp ground cloves
1 level tsp ground cinnamon
1 level tsp ground allspice

PREPARATION TIME: 15 minutes
MAKES: 1.1kg (2½lb)
PER SERVING: 65 cals, 2g fat, 12g carbohydrate

Kumquat mincemeat

1 Put the kumquats into a pan with the Grand Marnier and 150ml (¼ pint) water. Bring to the boil, then reduce the heat and simmer for 15 minutes or until tender. Remove kumquats with a slotted spoon and leave the liquid to cool.

2 Cut the apples in half, discarding pips, roughly chop and put into a large bowl. Add cooled liquid and remaining ingredients, and stir thoroughly.

3 Pack tightly into jars and cover as for jam. Store in a cool, dark place for up to 3 months.

225g (8oz) kumquats
150ml (¼ pint) Grand Marnier
225g (8oz) Bramley apples, cored and chopped
350g (12oz) each raisins, sultanas and currants
175g (6oz) each light and dark muscovado sugar
1 level tbsp ground mixed spice
pinch of ground nutmeg
grated zest and juice of 2 medium oranges

PREPARATION TIME: 15 minutes, plus cooling
COOKING TIME: 15 minutes
MAKES: about 1.6kg (3½lb)
PER SERVING: 70 cals, 0g fat, 17g carbohydrate

Drinks, liqueurs and bottled fruit

Fruits bottled with liqueur are some of the easiest and most tempting preserves to make, but they must be given plenty of time to mature. In some recipes the fruit is discarded once all its flavour has been absorbed into the alcohol, while in other recipes the fruit is served with the infused alcohol, either spooned over ice-cream or ladled out and topped with crème fraîche. Bottled fruits and syrups make lovely gifts as long you you're able to make them ahead of time so they're ready to enjoy once given. Autumn is a great time for making these preserves as they will then be ready for giving at Christmas. Fruit syrups and cordials are also easy to make and taste far better than bought ones. Sterilizing syrups and cordials, once bottled, have a storage life of between one and two months. Some can be made without sterilizing (such as ginger cordial), but their storage time in the fridge will be reduced to a couple of weeks. Wide-necked bottling jars are ideal for bottling whole fruits in alcohol (see page 8), but must be sterilized first. For cordials and syrup, bottles with rubber stoppers and clips are ideal. Again, these should be sterilized before use.

Clementines in Grand Marnier syrup

1   Using the tip of a small sharp knife, score a cross on the top and bottom of each clementine. Put them in a bowl and cover with boiling water. Set aside for 1 minute, then drain and peel the fruit. Carefully scrape away any pith from the fruit.

2   Put the sugar in a pan, then add the cinnamon stick, cloves and 300ml (½ pint) water. Heat the pan gently to dissolve the sugar, then increase the heat and bring the syrup to the boil. Simmer for 5 minutes.

3   Add the fruit and Grand Marnier to the pan and cook for a further 15–20 minutes. Remove from the heat and add the lemon juice.

4   Spoon the fruit into a 1 litre (1¾ pint) wide-necked jar, then pour the syrup over. Cover with the lid and cool. Store in the fridge for up to one month. Once open, keep in the fridge and use within 1 week.

10 clementines

175g (6oz) golden caster sugar

1 cinnamon stick

6 whole cloves

300ml (½ pint) Grand Marnier

juice of ½ lemon

PREPARATION TIME: 15 minutes

COOKING TIME: 20–25 minutes

MAKES: 1 litre (1¾ pints) (serves 10)

PER SERVING: 160 cals, 0g fat, 24g carbohydrate (per serving, including syrup)

Brandied cherries

1   Prick the cherries all over with a needle or fine skewer. Make a light syrup by dissolving 100g (4oz) of the sugar in 300ml (½ pint) water. Add the cherries and cinnamon stick and poach gently for 4–5 minutes.

2   Remove the pan from the heat and drain the cherries, reserving the syrup but removing the cinnamon stick. Cool, then arrange the fruit in small jars.

3   Add the remaining sugar to the reserved syrup and dissolve it slowly. Bring to the boil and boil to 110°C (230°F), then allow to cool before arranging the fruit in wide-necked jars.

4   Measure the syrup and add an equal quantity of brandy. Pour over the cherries and cover with the lid. Store in the fridge for up to 1 month. Once opened, use within a week.

450g (1lb) fresh cherries, washed
225g (8oz) sugar
1 cinnamon stick
about 150ml (¼ pint) brandy

PREPARATION TIME: 15 minutes, plus cooling
COOKING TIME: 15 minutes
MAKES: 450g (1lb)
PER SERVING: 140 cals, 0g fat, 29g carbohydrate

Orange liqueur

1   Peel the zest from the oranges in long, broad strips using a vegetable peeler.

2   Push the zest into two bottles and divide the wine, sugar and rum between them. Seal and shake well. Label and store for 6 weeks before drinking.

8 oranges, preferably unwaxed
1 bottle dry white wine
300 g (10 oz) golden caster sugar
600 ml (1 pint) white rum

PREPARATION TIME: 10 minutes
MAKES: 2 x 750ml (1¼ pint) bottles
PER SERVING: 100 cals, 0g fat, 11g carbohydrate per 50ml

Soft fruits in wine

1   Hull the strawberries, then halve and slice any large ones. Remove the redcurrants from their stalks. Wash and dry the fruit.

2   Place the sugar, wine and cardamom pods in a small saucepan. Heat gently, stirring occasionally, until the sugar has dissolved. Strain.

3   Layer the fruit in a large, wide-necked jar. When the fruit reaches the neck of the jar, fill it up with the red wine mixture. Screw the lid on tightly. Store in the fridge for 2–3 days before using. Use within 2 weeks.

900g (2lb) mixed soft red fruits, such as strawberries, redcurrants, raspberries
225g (8oz) caster sugar
½ bottle red wine
6 whole green cardamom pods, crushed

PREPARATION TIME: 10 minutes;
COOKING TIME: 3 minutes
MAKES: about 900g (2lb) (serves 10)
PER SERVING: 160 cals, 0g fat, 29g carbohydrate per portion

Sloe gin

1   Prick the sloes all over with a fine skewer or needle and put them in a screw-topped jar. Add the sugar and almond essence. Cover with gin, then screw down tightly. Leave in a dark place for 3 months, shaking occasionally.

2   Strain the gin through muslin until clear. Bottle the gin and store until required.

450g (1lb) sloes, stalks removed and washed
75–100g (3–4 oz) sugar
a few drops of almond essence
75cl (26.4 fl oz) bottle of gin

PREPARATION TIME: 15 minutes, plus standing
MAKES: 900ml (1½ pints)
PER SERVING: 110 cals, 0g fat, 5g carbohydrate per 50ml

Chardonnay pears

1   Put the pears and lemon juice in a bowl and toss to coat. Put to one side.

2   Put the sugar in a large pan, add the maple syrup, white wine, bay leaves and cinnamon stick and 300ml (½ pint) water. Heat gently to dissolve the sugar.

3   Add the pears and any juice to the pan, then bring to the boil, cover with greaseproof paper and a lid and simmer for 15–20 minutes, or until tender to the centre. The pears must be cooked through or they will discolour when stored.

4   Put the pears into wide-necked jars. Measure the liquid – there should be around 600ml (1 pint). If necessary, bring it to the boil and simmer to reduce, then leave to cool slightly.

5   Pour the syrup over the pears, making sure they are completely covered, then seal, label and store in the fridge. Use within 2 weeks.

8 medium, firm pears, peeled, halved and cored
juice of 1 large lemon
150g (5oz) golden granulated sugar
200ml (7fl oz) maple syrup
450ml (¾ pint) white wine, such as Chardonnay
3 fresh bay leaves
1 cinnamon stick

PREPARATION TIME: 20 minutes, plus cooling
COOKING TIME: 25 minutes
MAKES: 1 x 600ml (1 pint) jar and 1 x 1 litre (1¾ pint) jar
PER SERVING: 240 cals, 0g fat, 52g carbohydrate

Spiced pears in mulled wine

1   Mix together the honey, sugar, wine, cinnamon, orange rind and juice in a medium saucepan. Gently heat together until the sugar dissolves. Bring to the boil, then reduce to a simmer.

2   Meanwhile, peel the pears with a vegetable peeler, leaving the stalks intact to make them easier to handle. Cut a thin slice from the base of each pear so that it sits upright. Lower into the wine.

3   Add just enough water to cover the pears and set a heatproof plate on top to keep them immersed in the liquid. Poach the pears at a gentle simmer for 20–25 minutes until tender (test by piercing with a knife).

4   Lift the cooked pears from the pan and place in wide-necked jars. Put the saucepan back on the hob, bring to the boil and bubble for 15–20 minutes until the syrup has reduced and is syrupy – the time with depend on how much water was added to cover the pears. Strain the wine over the pears to colour them evenly, then cover with the lid. Use within two weeks.

Note
Firm pears such as comice and conference are best for poaching. Try other spices in the syrup, such as sliced fresh root ginger or whole cloves.

6 tbsp honey

6 tbsp light muscovado sugar

300ml (½ pint) full-bodied, fruity red wine

1 cinnamon stick or large pinch of ground cinnamon

Pared rind and juice of 1 large orange

6 small pears, ripe but firm

PREPARATION TIME: 15 minutes
COOKING TIME: 40–45 minutes
MAKES: 6 servings
PER SERVING: 200 cals, 0g fat, 43g carbohydrate

Brandied peaches

1   If using fresh peaches, skin the peaches by plunging them into boiling water, then gently peeling off the skins. Halve the peaches and remove the stones.

2   Make a light syrup by dissolving 100g (4oz) of the sugar in 300ml (½ pint) water. Add the peaches and poach gently for 4–5 minutes.

3   Remove the pan from the heat, drain the peaches, reserving the syrup. Leave to cool. Arrange the fruit in wide-necked jars.

4   Add the remaining sugar to the reserved syrup and dissolve it slowly. Bring it to the boil and boil to 110°C (90°C fan) ½ mark, then allow to cool.

5   Measure the syrup and add an equal quantity of brandy or liqueur. Pour over the peaches and cover with the lids. Leave for 2–3 months before eating.

6   If using canned peaches, drain the syrup from the peaches and put in a saucepan (this size of can yields about 450ml / ¾ pint syrup). Reduce the syrup to half the quantity by boiling gently, remove from the heat and leave to cool.

7   Prick the peaches with a fine skewer or needle and place in wide-necked jars. Add brandy or liqueur to the syrup and pour over the fruit. Cover with lids.

450g (1lb) fresh peaches or one
  822g (1lb 13oz) can peach
  halves
225g (8oz) sugar (if using fresh
  peaches)
about 150ml (¼ pint) brandy or
  orange flavoured liqueur

PREPARATION TIME: 10 minutes,
plus cooling
COOKING TIME: 15 minutes
MAKES: 450g (1lb)
PER SERVING: 170 cals, 0g fat, 34g
carbohydrate

Hot chilli vodka

1 Split the chillies lengthways. Mix with the vodka in a bottle with a tight-fitting lid.

2 Shake and leave in a cool place for at least 2 weeks before using. Store for up to 3 months.

Variation: citrus vodka
This produces a pale lemon-coloured spirit. Try adding a little to sautés of beef or chicken, or stir a couple of spoonfuls into fruit salads or over slices of fresh pineapple. Omit the chillies from the above recipe and add the pared rind of 3 lemons.

Variation: pepper vodka
Omit the chillies from the above recipe and add 2 level tbsp lightly crushed green peppercorns. This variation is also delicious served in a Bloody Mary.

1 red and 1 green chilli
300ml (½ pint) vodka

PREPARATION TIME: 5 minutes;
MAKES: 300ml (½ pint)
PER SERVING: 110 cals, 0g fat, 0g carbohydrate

Cassis

1 Crush the blackcurrants. Place with the gin or brandy in screw-topped jars, then screw down tightly. Leave in a dark place for about 2 months.

2 Strain the spirit, then add 175g (6oz) sugar to each 600ml (1 pint) liquid. Pour into a jug, cover and leave for 2 days, stirring at intervals to dissolve the sugar. Strain through muslin. Bottle the liqueur and store for 6 months to mature before using.

450g (1lb) blackcurrants, stalks removed and washed
600ml (1 pint) gin or brandy
sugar

PREPARATION TIME: 10 minutes, plus standing
MAKES: 1.1 litres (2 pints)
PER SERVING: 160 cals, 0g fat, 14g carbohydrate

Lemon squash

1   Grate the rind of two lemons and squeeze out the juice from all the fruit to make 300ml (½ pint) juice. Place the lemon rind, sugar and 450ml (¾ pint) water in a saucepan and heat slowly until boiling, stirring until the sugar has dissolved.

2   Strain the syrup into a jug, add the lemon juice and citric acid, if used, and stir well. Pour into bottles, seal and sterilize.

3   To serve, dilute the squash with water or soda water – allow I part squash to 20 parts water, according to taste. Do not store for longer than I–2 months, as the colour and flavour deteriorate.

about 7 lemons, washed
700g (1½ lb) sugar
1.25 ml (¼ tsp) citric acid (optional)

PREPARATION TIME: 10 minutes
COOKING TIME: about 5 minutes
MAKES: 900ml (1½ pints)
PER SERVING: 30 cals, 0g fat, 8g carbohydrate

Orange squash

1   Grate the rind of the oranges, squeeze out the juice and measure 300ml (½ pint) juice.

2   Place the orange rind, sugar and 450ml (¾ pint) water in a saucepan and heat slowly until boiling, stirring until the sugar has dissolved.

3   Strain the syrup into a jug, add the orange juice and citric acid, and stir well. Pour into bottles, seal and sterilize.

4   To serve, dilute with water or soda water – allow I part squash to 2–3 parts water, according to taste. Do not store for longer than I–2 months, as the colour and flavour deteriorate.

about 4 oranges, washed
700g (1½ lb) sugar
15g (½ oz) citric acid

PREPARATION TIME: 10 minutes
COOKING TIME: about 5 minutes
MAKES: 900ml (1½ pints)
PER SERVING: 30 cals, 0g fat, 8g carbohydrate

Ginger cordial

1   Put the ginger, sugar, tartaric acid and lemon in a large bowl. Cover with 2.4 litres (4 pints) boiling water, stir until the sugar has dissolved, then leave for 3–4 days in a cool place.

2   Strain the cordial through muslin, then pour into bottles, seal and sterilize. This cordial is ready to drink, undiluted, after a few days. Chill before serving.

50g (2oz) peeled fresh root ginger, grated
225g (8oz) granulated sugar
1 level tsp tartaric acid
½ a lemon, washed and sliced

PREPARATION TIME: 10 minutes, plus standing
MAKES: about 2.4 litres (4 pints)
PER SERVING: 20 cals, 0g fat, 6g carbohydrate per 50ml

Elderflower cordial

1   Place all the ingredients in a bowl. Cover and leave for 24 hours, stirring occasionally.

2   Strain the cordial through muslin, pour into bottles, seal and sterilize. To serve, dilute to taste with sparkling mineral water.

10 large elderflower heads
900g (2lb) sugar
2 lemons, washed and sliced
25g (1oz) tartaric acid
2.4 litres (4 pints) boiling water

PREPARATION TIME: 10 minutes, plus standing
MAKES: about 2 litres (3½ pints)
PER SERVING: 25 cals, 0g fat, 7g carbohydrate per tsp

Blackcurrant and rosemary syrup

1   Place the blackcurrants in a medium saucepan with the rosemary and 300ml (½ pint) water. Bring slowly to the boil and simmer for 5 minutes or until the fruit is very soft and pulpy.

2   Press the mixture through a nylon sieve, extracting all the liquid. Measure the liquid into a small saucepan. Add 150g (5oz) caster sugar and the juice of 1 lemon to each 600ml (1 pint).

3   Heat the mixture gently, stirring, until the sugar has dissolved, then bring to the boil and boil for 10 minutes or until syrupy.

4   Pour the syrup into clean, warmed bottles and seal. Cool, label and store in a cool, dark place for up to 1 month.

900g (2lb) blackcurrants, stalks
    removed and washed
2 sprigs of fresh rosemary
caster sugar
lemon juice

PREPARATION TIME: 10 minutes
COOKING TIME: about 20 minutes
MAKES: about 600ml (1 pint)
PER SERVING: 25 cals, 0g fat, 7g
carbohydrate per tsp

Rosehip syrup

1   Have ready 1.7 litres (3 pints) boiling water, in a large saucepan.

2   Press the rosehips through the coarse blade of a mincer and place immediately in the boiling water. Bring to the boil again. As soon as the mixture boils, remove the pan from the heat and leave for 15 minutes.

3   Pour the rosehips into a scalded jelly bag and allow the bulk of the juice to drip through.

4   Return the pulp in the jelly bag to the saucepan, add 900ml (1½ pints) boiling water, re-boil, then allow to stand without further heating for another 10 minutes.

5   Pour the juice into a clean saucepan and simmer to reduce to about 900ml (1½ pints), then add 450g (1lb) sugar. Stir until dissolved, then boil for a further 5 minutes.

6   Pour the hot syrup into hot bottles and seal at once. Sterilize for 5 minutes.

Note

It is advisable to use small bottles, as the syrup will not keep for more than a week or two once it is opened.

900g (2lb) ripe rosehips
450g (1lb) sugar

PREPARATION TIME: 20 minutes, plus standing
COOKING TIME: 15 minutes
MAKES: 600ml (1 pint)
PER SERVING: 45 cals, 0g fat, 2g carbohydrate per tsp

Problem-solving

Fruit or peel floating to the top

If most of the fruit rises to the top of the jam once the heat is turned off, leave it to cool for 15 minutes before potting. Give it a good stir first so that the fruit disperses itself in the syrup. Always leave marmalade to stand before potting, so that the peel evenly disperses.

Mould forming on surface

A thin layer, or patches of greyish white mould forming on top of potted preserves is caused either by potting while warm (rather than piping hot or cold), using unsterilized jars or storing the jam in too warm an environment. Open the pots, remove the mould and a thick layer off the surface of the jam. Transfer to the fridge for storage.

Crystallization

Caused by using too much sugar, or not dissolving it sufficiently before bringing the preserve to the boil. This cannot be remedied after potting and although still edible, will have a rather crunchy texture.

Tough marmalade peel

Peel not sufficiently softened in the juice before adding the sugar. This cannot be remedied once the marmalade is made so check that the peel is very soft before adding the sugar.

Shrinking away from sides of jar

This is caused by over boiling or not creating an airtight seal when covering the jars. Re-cover the jars to prevent further evaporation.

Problems when setting

If the preserve shows no signs of setting when the estimated boiling time is reached, remove from the heat and add 2 teaspoons of citric or tartaric acid. Lemon juice can be used instead but the liquid will further thin the jam. Re-boil the jam before testing for a set.

Bubbles dispersed in jellies

Caused through leaving the jelly too long before potting so the jelly has over thickened, trapping bubbles of air. Scum that hasn't been removed prior to potting will also spoil the appearance of a jelly.

Dull colours in jams

This is usually caused through overcooking, either before adding the sugar or during boiling.

Fermentation of mincemeat

If jars start oozing syrup, this is usually a sign of fermentation, caused by inaccurate weighing of ingredients e.g. insufficient sugar, not enough lemon juice or inclusion of too many sweet rather than sour apples. Poor storage might also cause fermentation. If this happens, boil up the mincemeat in a saucepan and pot into sterilized jars. Store in the fridge.

Drying out

If the surface of the mincemeat is very dry, stir in a little alcohol such as brandy, or the type used in the original recipe.

Index